Perfect Family Quiz

David Pickering is an enthusiastic quiz team member as well as an experienced reference book compiler, having contributed to some 150 reference books, mostly in the areas of the arts, language, local history and popular interest. These include an *Encyclopedia of Pantomime* (1993), a *Soccer Companion* (1994; 1997), a *Dictionary of Superstitions* (1995), a *Dictionary of Witchcraft* (1996) and a *Dictionary of Proverbs* (2001; 2003). He is also the author of *Perfect Pub Quiz* (2007). He lives in Buckingham with his wife and two sons.

Other titles in the *Perfect* series

Perfect
Family Quiz

David Pickering

BOOKS

Published by Random House Books 2009

8 10 9 7

First published in Great Britain in 2009 by
Random House Books

Random House, 20 Vauxhall Bridge Road,
London SW1V 2SA
www.rbooks.co.uk

Addresses for companies within The Random House Group Limited
can be found at: www.randomhouse.co.uk/offices.htm

The Random House Group Limited Reg. No. 954009

A CIP catalogue record for this book
is available from the British Library

ISBN 9781847945297

The Random House Group Limited supports The Forest Stewardship
Council (FSC), the leading international forest certification organisation.
All our titles that are printed on Greenpeace approved FSC certified paper
carry the FSC logo. Our paper procurement policy can be found at
www.randomhouse.co.uk/environment

Typeset by SX Composing DTP, Rayleigh, Essex
Printed and bound by CPI Group (UK) Ltd, Croydon, CR0 4YY

Contents

The author would like to dedicate this book to the many members of his own extended Perfect Family. He would also like to thank Sophie Lazar and Emily Rhodes at Random House Books for their patient assistance.

While every effort has been made to ensure that the information contained in this book is accurate, there must always remain the possibility of there being the odd inaccuracy, for which the author blames himself for not knowing better.

Introduction

The quiz has long been an established favourite of family entertainment. Thousands of families gathered together at Christmas time, or on holiday, or just seeking a pleasant means to while away an evening enjoying something everyone can take part in, have reached for a quiz in a magazine or in a book like this one. Few quizzes, however, cater for all the varied age groups within the typical family: children tire of questions that they think too difficult, while adults soon weary of questions that they find too easy. This book seeks to provide a solution, mixing questions of varying difficulty together, allowing everyone a chance to shine.

The quizzes in this book include a wide variety of types of question, from straightforward tests of general knowledge to multiple choice and true-or-false posers. Each quiz begins and ends with a pot luck round covering a random selection of themes and is completed by two specialist rounds as well as a half-time teaser and jackpot question. Subjects covered in the specialist rounds include all manner of topics, from current affairs, history, arts and culture, science and nature to television, children's toys, sport, people and places. Easier questions are mixed throughout with harder ones, meaning that everyone has a chance of knowing an answer, whatever their age and ability.

In this introduction, I've made some suggestions on how to personalise your quiz, with tips on how to write your own rounds – from up-to-the-minute current affairs questions to music and picture rounds. You'll also find some useful hints on how to run a quiz, from choosing teams to working out the scores.

The first hundred quizzes are general (although there is a list of rounds sorted by theme at the end of this introduction). These are followed by a further ten quizzes aimed at specific age groups.

How to use this book

This book offers a complete quiz of thirty questions on each double-page spread. Quizmasters may choose to deliver the quizzes as presented, complete with half-time teaser and jackpot question (and perhaps with the addition of their own interval round) or else select rounds from different quizzes and compile their own combination of questions. Of course, there is absolutely no reason why enthusiastic quiz players should not use the book simply to test their own knowledge or to brush up their question-answering skills for the future.

Half-time teasers

After the first two rounds, there is a half-time teaser, often comprising a physical challenge of some kind, designed particularly to spark the interest of younger participants.

Jackpot questions

Many of the hardest questions are reserved for the jackpot round (though some are easier than others, and a question is only hard if you don't know the answer). Virtually all of these include a choice of answers, so even if you're not sure of the answer you still have a chance of winning with a lucky (or educated) guess. There are various ways in which the jackpot question can be used. It can be employed to settle the final result of the quiz or, alternatively, it can be offered as a separate question after the rest of the quiz has been decided, with (perhaps) its own special prize.

Fascinating facts

Another unique feature of this book is the addition of a fascinating fact relating to one question in each quiz. Indicated by an asterisk (*) after the question, such glosses are designed purely for the enjoyment and elucidation of quizmaster and contestants alike. If the sharing of such priceless information allows the quizmaster to look much cleverer and well-informed than he or she really this, this is entirely intentional!∗

∗ Did you know, for instance, that the word 'quiz' came about as the result of a bet? When the eighteenth-century Irish theatre manager James Daly was wagered that he could not make a new word catch on in a single day, he travelled all over Dublin writing the mysterious word 'quiz' on walls – with the result that soon everyone was talking about it and the word itself entered the language.

Adding your own touches

A single quiz from this book may take anything from half an hour to an hour to complete, depending upon the ages of those taking part and whether it has been agreed to write answers down or not. Either way, this allows plenty of time for quizmasters, if they wish, to insert a round of their own devising, perhaps when the quiz reaches the halfway stage.

Such interval rounds provide quizmasters with the opportunity of expanding the range of questions by introducing a set of self-compiled questions that may have particular relevance to the people taking part or the occasion on which the quiz participants have gathered. Alternatively, these questions may deal with topical events that inevitably cannot be covered in a book such as this.

Points won during this round may be added to the overall total, or else treated separately and rewarded (at the quizmaster's discretion) with a special prize.

There are numerous possibilities for interval rounds, but the following pages suggest just a few ideas that might inspire quizmasters to think about adding a round or two of their own devising.

Current affairs quiz rounds

Although every effort has been made to introduce plenty of recent material in questions for this book, quiz players are usually surprised and entertained to be asked questions about events that have taken place in the last few weeks, days or even hours. Ideas for possible questions on such diverse topics as the news of the day, sport, gossip, television and the royal family quickly suggest themselves from a cursory read of the day's newspapers or through other branches of the media. A few carefully chosen questions on current affairs arranged on the pattern of other rounds in this book are sure to go down well.

Local knowledge quiz rounds

Questions based on the immediate surroundings of the place where the quiz is taking place are always fun. Such questions are beyond the scope of this book, but may prove a very popular choice for interval rounds. Consider compiling a round of questions that test the local knowledge of those present – but try not to get too bogged down in questions that focus primarily on local history: there are many other kinds of questions that may be asked about the typical town or village, as the following suggestions indicate.

What is the name of the river that flows through the town?
Which school stands at [location]?
What would you buy at [name of local store]?
Whose statue stands in [location]?
What disaster befell the people of the town in [date]?
Which [animal, symbol, etc.] is featured on the town crest?
Which celebrity was born in [local place]?
What is the name of our twin town in [country]?
Which day of the week is market day?
Which king or queen stayed in the town in [date]?
Which pub is located in [name of street]?
What colour strip does the town's football team play in?

Music quiz rounds

One of the most popular of optional interval rounds is the music quiz round. These can range from straightforward questions about music and musicians of all kinds to challenges to identify excerpts of particular songs or other musical works.

Perhaps the most entertaining way to organise an interval music round is to record the opening notes or bars of a piece of music and then challenge players to identify the piece and the performers or composer (or even all three). Alternatively, vary the formula by asking for the year in which a song was released, or reached number one, etc. In many cases it is possible to play the whole opening verse of a song before the chorus gives the game away. In others, a single note provides a sufficient clue. Preparing such a round may be fairly time-consuming, and organising something to play the clips on may be an issue, but the result usually makes the effort worthwhile.

Picture quiz rounds

Another great favourite is the picture quiz round, which can take a number of different forms. One that goes down particularly well is the challenge to identify pictures of celebrities of various kinds, disguised by showing only part of their face or showing them in an out-of-character context or at an odd angle or even with beards and moustaches drawn on their photograph. All the quizmaster needs to do is find suitable pictures of ten or more well-known people, cut them out as desired, paste them onto a piece of paper, number them, and then photocopy the sheet for all the players attending, who must match each number with the correct name.

Alternative versions of the picture quiz round might involve players identifying places (perhaps in the town where they live) through pictures of distinctive architectural details etc. Particularly ambitious quizmasters may like to compile sets of three or four pictures and challenge players to identify the link between them (for instance, pictures of a red squirrel, a football player wearing red, a Red Army flag and one of the RAF Red Arrow aeroplanes – 'red' being the link).

Atlas rounds

There are many imaginative optional rounds that a quizmaster can construct based on photocopied pages from an atlas (preferably one that presents just outlines of countries etc. and little written information). These may relate to the whole world, a continent or just a single country, such as the UK. The players may then be challenged to identify marked countries, towns, islands, mountains, seaside resorts, rivers, or a host of other features. Alternatively, draw a line between two locations in different parts of the world and challenge the players to identify all the countries, states or counties that a person would go through if flying directly between the two places (a line taking in the newer countries of south-east Europe or the states of the central USA would certainly test most people).

Name the year rounds

Name the year rounds are an alternative for interval rounds with which most quiz players will be familiar. The usual option is to list three contrasting events of major or minor importance and challenge players to guess the year. To make things a little easier, the quizmaster might offer leeway of a year either side. Such rounds work best when all the players are adults.

Matching pairs rounds

These rounds comprise two lists of items that players have to match up correctly. The difficulty of such rounds is up to the quizmaster. Players may find it relatively easy to match famous husbands and wives or inventions with inventors, for instance, but much harder to pair up car models with manufacturers or battles with the wars they occurred in. The possibilities are endless – players may be asked to pair sports teams with their nicknames, football teams with their grounds, artists with masterpieces, singers with hit songs, comedians with their partners, film stars with films, detectives with their assistants, sailors with their ships, people with their animals, companies with their logos, etc. etc. etc.

Running a quiz

To run a successful quiz, more is required than just a set of questions and answers (as provided by this book). Having got everyone comfortable, the quizmaster (or the players themselves) needs to decide if people are to play separately or in teams. If there is a wide range of ages involved, it is usually sensible to organise teams in which the ages are thoroughly mixed, younger players with older players, rather than to have children playing against adults, for instance. Pencils and paper will be needed if answers are to be written down, and some of the half-time teasers require the use of a coin or other similar everyday item. A sample answer sheet suitable for photocopying may be found at the end of this book.

Each team must choose a name and write this on their answer sheet. Quizmasters must make sure that everyone understands the way the quiz will work and whether jackpot questions will be used to decide the result in the event of a draw.

Scoring

The easiest way to score is to reward each correct answer with one point, the total being added up after all the answers have been announced. Quizmasters may, of course, elect to award double points for their own interval rounds if they so wish. One option is to tot up scores after each round, as this can increase the tension as players see how they are faring against each other. This also works best if jokers are to be employed (a joker being the option of each player or team to choose one round in which every correct answer they give is rewarded with double points). When totting up points at the end, incidentally, it can be advisable to get teams to swap answer sheets and then to double-check the winning sheet before announcing the final result.

Themed rounds

Players may show interest in answering questions on particular subjects, in which case the following list of themed rounds from the 100 general quizzes contained within the book may be useful. This list may also be useful if a quizmaster wants to tailor a quiz to appeal to a particular age group, gender, etc. The numbers given relate to the quizzes where the questions can be found.

Animals (1, 5, 7, 17, 23, 45, 47, 58, 62, 71, 78, 85, 92, 98)
Art (23)
Beliefs and Superstitions (10, 63, 75)
Bells and Whistles (95)
Big Bangs (60)
Birds (41, 74)
Books (6)
Buildings (81, 83, 86)
Cartoons (21)
Catchphrases (36, 55, 89)
Celebrities (50)
Changes (64)
Clothes and Fashion (6, 31, 67, 77)
Colours (11, 66, 72, 97)
Connections (39)
Cowboys (38)
Crime (2, 22, 29, 45, 90)
Dance (79)
Days of the Week (87)
Disasters (20)
Explorers (14, 78)
Fairy Tales (19)
Families (8, 80)
Fictional Characters (25, 26, 68)
Films (4, 48, 65, 84)
Fire and Water (57)

Turn to the age-specific quizzes at the end of the book for further rounds on such themes as royalty, the war years, rock and roll, indoor games, soap operas, cookery, clothing and fashion, sports, films, books, wild animals, fairy tales and nursery rhymes.

Perfect
Family Quiz

Quiz 1

Round 1: Pot Luck

1 Who lives at 10 Downing Street?

2 Who followed Pierce Brosnan as James Bond in 2006?

3 In which country is the didgeridoo a traditional instrument?

4 In *Cinderella*, what was turned into a coach to take Cinders to the ball?

5 Whereabouts in Europe is the Blarney Stone?

6 Who was Elizabeth I's father?

7 Which is the largest island in the world that is not a continent?

Round 2: Four-legged Friends

1 What is Mickey Mouse's dog called?

2 What kind of animal ate Red Riding Hood's grandmother?

3 What is the male equivalent of a filly?

4 Are porcupines a variety of rodent, rabbit or badger?

5 Which is the odd one out – saddleback, palomino or Gloucestershire old spot?

6 Which animal resembling a hairy elephant died out in the last Ice Age?

7 Which creature comes in black, brown and kangaroo varieties?

Half-time teaser

For an extra point, who can repeat 'How much wood would a woodchuck chuck if a woodchuck could chuck wood?' the fastest, three times, without making a mistake?

Round 3: Kids' TV

1 Which of the following is not a Teletubby – Dizzy, Tinky Winky, Laa Laa or Po?

2 Christopher Trace, Caron Keating and Konnie Huq have all been presenters of which programme?

3 What is the name of Malcolm's dad in *Malcolm in the Middle*?

4 Who was the usual pilot of Thunderbird 1?

5 The end of which long-running drama series set in a school was announced in 2008?

6 Which children's cartoon series is set in Bikini Bottom?

7 The Soup Dragon was a character in which classic kids' TV series?

Round 4: Pot Luck

1 Which is greater, ten times one hundred or one hundred times ten?

2 An ugli fruit is the result of a cross between a tangerine and which other fruit?

3 In which sequence of novels is Frodo a central character?

4 What is dermatology the study of?

5 The film *Amadeus* was about which composer?

6 Which country is home to a football team called Juventus?

7 What colour is Sonic the Hedgehog?

Jackpot

In which year did Paris became the first city to give houses numbers – 1463, 1663 or 1863? ✳

✳ London copied the idea 300 years later.

Quiz 2

Round 1: Pot Luck

1 How do you spell 'wriggle'?

2 Which is an item of clothing – a cagoule, a kayak or a canoe?

3 Who was the emperor of Japan during World War II?

4 In Australian slang, what is a dunny?

5 What is the Russian name for an astronaut?

6 Which emotion is sometimes represented as a green-eyed monster?

7 On which fictional island do the *Thomas the Tank Engine* stories take place?

Round 2: Notorious Murders

1 Who killed Cock Robin?

2 In which US city did the St Valentine's Day massacre of 1929 take place?

3 Who was king at the time of the murder of Thomas Becket – Henry II, Richard III or Henry VIII?

4 In which city did William Burke and William Hare murder people to provide surgeons with bodies?

5 What was the name of the Scottish king murdered by Shakespeare's Macbeth?

6 Which member of the Beatles was murdered in New York in 1980?

7 In which US city was President John F. Kennedy assassinated in 1963?

Half-time teaser

For the youngest members of each team: For an extra point, who can recite the alphabet backwards without making a mistake?

QUIZZES 5

Round 3: Science and Technology

1 Which branch of science deals with the study of living things?
2 What is measured in decibels?
3 With which branch of the sciences was the Greek Hippocrates associated?
4 In which country did the R101 airship crash?
5 *Heathen Chemistry* and *Definitely Maybe* are albums by which rock band?
6 At what temperature Celsius does water boil?
7 What was the name of the famous locomotive designed by George and Robert Stephenson in 1829?

Round 4: Pot Luck

1 Who was the Norse god of thunder?
2 What is a tsunami?
3 Which is larger – Canada or Europe?
4 Which motoring programme is presented by Jeremy Clarkson, Richard Hammond and James May?
5 In 2000 Craig Phillips was the first UK winner of which television reality show?
6 Hummingbirds cannot walk – true or false?
7 What is the last word in the New Testament?

Jackpot

The French Revolution took place in which year – 1689, 1789 or 1889?

✻ The Rev. W. Awdry, who wrote the stories, provided full details of the island, which he imagined as lying between the real Isle of Man and mainland England. A road bridge connects the island railway system with the mainland network at Barrow-in-Furness.

Quiz 3

Round 1: Pot Luck

1 Which animal comes in grey and timber varieties?

2 Sark is part of which island group?

3 What kind of animal is the master criminal Feathers McGraw in *The Wrong Trousers*?

4 What term describes a person who is equally skilful with both hands?

5 Who has a girlfriend called Olive Oyl?

6 What is the name of the huge Antony Gormley statue that stands beside the A1 near Gateshead?

7 Who was known as the Nine Days' Queen?

Round 2: Sporty Types

1 W. G. Grace was a legendary figure in which sport – rugby, golf or cricket?

2 With which Premier League club did England captain Alan Shearer end his career?

3 How many events are there in a decathlon?

4 Which county cricket team play at Trent Bridge?

5 With which sport was Colin McRae associated?

6 Which is the odd one out – niblick, tee, green, fairground?

7 In which city is the Murrayfield rugby stadium?

Half-time teaser

For an extra point, who can give the best impression of Donald Duck?

Round 3: Clever Notions

1 What did Igor Sikorsky invent in 1939?

2 Which children's toy comprises a metal spring capable of climbing down stairs?

3 Leonardo da Vinci produced designs for a hang-glider – true or false?

4 In which year was the first colour photograph taken – 1861, 1901 or 1931? ✶

5 Which was invented first – the aeroplane or the parachute?

6 What can a polygraph do?

7 Which computer company founded by Bill Gates made him the richest man in the world?

Round 4: Pot Luck

1 Who had a sword called Excalibur?

2 By what other name do Americans refer to the 'Sasquatch'?

3 Which anniversary marks forty years of married life?

4 Which of the world's countries has the largest area?

5 What green-coloured substance is supposedly fatal to Superman?

6 In the Tom and Jerry cartoons, what kind of animal is Jerry?

7 Which gemstone consists of fossilised resin?

Jackpot

How long does an average person spend dreaming each night – two minutes, twenty minutes or two hours?

✶The very first colour photograph, taken by Scotsman James Clerk Maxwell, was of a piece of tartan ribbon. It is preserved today in Maxwell's house, now a small museum, in Edinburgh.

Quiz 4

Round 1: Pot Luck

1 A starfish has no brain – true or false?

2 In ancient times, what was a bireme – a ship, a hairstyle or something you ate?

3 Where might one find a level crossing?

4 What is a balalaika – a horsedrawn carriage, a musical instrument or a dance?

5 Who was the first person to reach the South Pole?

6 What is the Old Bailey – a pub, a theatre or a court?

7 Which animals come in moray, electric and conger varieties?

Round 2: At the Movies

1 Hollywood is a suburb of which US city?

2 Who sang the theme song for the James Bond film *Tomorrow Never Dies*?

3 Macaulay Culkin played Kevin McCallister in which film series?

4 In which Disney movie does the song 'Hakuna matata' feature?

5 In the *Star Wars* films, who is the commander of the Millennium Falcon?

6 Which was Adolf Hitler's favourite movie – *Gone with the Wind*, *The Dambusters* or *King Kong*?

7 Which Scottish hero was played by Mel Gibson in *Braveheart*?

Half-time teaser

For an extra point, who can hum for the longest without a break?

Round 3: Around Britain

1 Whereabouts in the UK is the Giant's Causeway?

2 Which English forest is said to have been home to the outlaw Robin Hood?

3 In which year did Wales acquire a National Assembly – 1979, 1989 or 1999?

4 In which part of the UK is the ceilidh (pronounced 'kaylee') a traditional form of entertainment?

5 In which city is the famous Spaghetti Junction network of roads?

6 Great Paul is a large bell in which British cathedral?

7 The Fens are located where – Cornwall, Wales or East Anglia?

Round 4: Pot Luck

1 Bladderwrack is a form of what?

2 What is the seventeenth letter of the alphabet?

3 Which parts of the body does a manicurist treat?

4 In which year did the £1 note cease to be legal tender in the UK – 1984, 1988 or 1992?

5 For which foodstuff is the French town of Dijon famous?

6 What lethal weapon was invented in the French town of Bayonne?

7 Who was British prime minister at the start of World War II?

Jackpot

What percentage of people in the world are estimated never to have used a telephone – 10 per cent, 25 per cent or 50 per cent?

✶Director George Lucas said that the design of the Millennium Falcon was suggested by the shape of a hamburger, with the cockpit on the side being suggested by an olive.

Quiz 5

Round 1: Pot Luck

1 What is the Queen's London home?

2 What is 25 per cent as a fraction?

3 Which member of the original *Star Trek* crew was born on the planet Vulcan?

4 How many points does a snooker player get for potting the black ball?

5 What was the Conservative party originally known as?

6 Which classic TV series featured the World Aquanaut Security Patrol?

7 What kind of animal is a featherfin squeaker – a fish, a bird or a beetle?

Round 2: Creepy-crawlies

1 What does a lepidopterist collect?

2 How many pairs of legs do all insects have?

3 Which has more muscles – a human or a caterpillar?

4 Who swallowed a spider to catch a fly?

5 Which part of an insect connects its head with its abdomen?

6 What is the larval form of a housefly called?

7 Butterflies taste things with their feet – true or false?

Half-time teaser

For an extra point, who can sing the highest note?

Round 3: Fruit and Veg

1 According to the proverb, an apple a day keeps who away?

2 Is a peanut a pea, a nut or a seed?

3 Which shredded vegetable is the main ingredient of sauerkraut?

4 Failure of which crop caused famine in Ireland in the 1840s?

5 Which pop star has a daughter named Peaches?

6 Which type of fruit first went on sale in Britain on 10 April 1633?

7 Eating which vegetable is traditionally supposed to aid eyesight?

Round 4: Pot Luck

1 What is Paddington Bear's favourite food? *

2 Who was spied on by Peeping Tom in 1040?

3 Dentophobia is the fear of what?

4 The Bayeux Tapestry depicts what series of historical events?

5 In a Roman house, what was the *triclinium*?

6 Over which South American people did Atahualpa reign?

7 What colour do you get if you mix blue and yellow?

Jackpot

When did the Great Train Robbery take place – 1953, 1963 or 1973?

* The answer is not Marmite, even though Paddington appeared in a series of adverts in 2007 enjoying Marmite for a change from his usual favourite. Paddington's creator, Michael Bond, criticised the campaign, about which he had not been consulted.

Quiz 6

Round 1: Pot Luck

1 Which three colours appear on the Union flag of the United Kingdom?

2 What is the name of the lovestruck bellringer in Victor Hugo's *The Hunchback of Notre Dame*?

3 What kind of shelter do pet rabbits usually live in?

4 Which are more popular – blue toothbrushes or red toothbrushes?

5 What is a mamba – a snake, a dance or a small car?

6 Which queen was known as 'Gloriana'?

7 What gender are worker ants?

Round 2: Brilliant Books

1 In *The Jungle Book*, what is Bagheera?

2 What does the author of an autobiography write about?

3 Who created the fictional butler Jeeves?

4 Which book begins: 'Lyra and her daemon moved through the darkening Hall, taking care to keep to one side, out of sight of the kitchen'?

5 For what series of books did Terry Deary become well known?

6 *War and Peace* was written by which great Russian novelist?

7 In which book do five children meet a creature called the Psammead?

Half-time teaser

For an extra point, can you write the word 'received', correctly spelled?

Round 3: The Rag Trade

1 Thomas Hancock invented elastic in which year – 1820, 1880 or 1920?

2 In which country is the sari a traditional form of dress?

3 Where might one wear a homburg?

4 In Cockney rhyming slang, what is a 'dicky dirt'?

5 What comes in Norfolk, Argyll and flak varieties?

6 Where is a sporran part of the national costume?

7 For whom are most romper suits made?

Round 4: Pot Luck

1 Who is the patron saint of England?

2 Which London building is famous for its Whispering Gallery?

3 In which sport was Alain Prost a champion?

4 Which of the following animals is never mentioned in the Bible – a sheep, a cat or a goat?

5 Which sea lies between Britain and Denmark?

6 In which country was Eva Perón a national figurehead?

7 Which of the following is not a size of bottle –Botticelli, Methuselah or Jeroboam?

Jackpot

In which year did Smarties first go on sale – 1907, 1937 or 1957? *

* Blue-coloured Smarties were introduced in 1988, replacing light brown Smarties, but they were removed in 2006 because the blue dye relied on unhealthy artificial colouring. They were briefly replaced by white Smarties, until the blue ones were reintroduced in 2008, using a natural blue seaweed dye.

Quiz 7

Round 1: Pot Luck

1 The Statue of Liberty stands outside which city?

2 How many hulls does a catamaran have?

3 What is the name of the city in which the medical drama series *Casualty* is set?

4 Latvia and Lithuania are two of the Baltic states – which is the third?

5 Which football team play at the Madejski Stadium?

6 There are no penguins at the North Pole – true or false?

7 In which country can one see the Great Sphinx?

Round 2: Sea Life

1 Which has more tentacles – an octopus or a squid?

2 Which kind of sea creature comes in grey, monk and leopard varieties?

3 Grog, traditionally served to members of the Royal Navy, was a mixture of rum and what?

4 What is a stickleback – a kind of turtle, a hedgehog or a small fish?

5 What does a narwhal have that makes it unique among whales?

6 How many pairs of legs, including the claws, do most crabs have?

7 What is the name of the ghostly galleon said to bring bad luck to all who see her? *

Half-time teaser

For an extra point, who can list the most countries beginning with the letter C?

Round 3: Pop Stars

1 Whose first album was called *Baby One More Time*?

2 Who topped the British singles charts for ten weeks in 2007 singing about an umbrella?

3 Which pop group did Robbie Williams leave in 1995?

4 Of what instrument was Jimi Hendrix a master?

5 Which Lewis released *Spirit*, the fastest selling debut album of all time, in 2007?

6 What is Kylie Minogue's middle name – Joan, Phyllis or Ann?

7 Which pop star has the nickname 'Material Girl'?

Round 4: Pot Luck

1 Who had an assistant called Dr Watson?

2 With whom did Shakespeare's Romeo fall in love?

3 From which Mediterranean island did the emperor Napoleon escape in 1815?

4 What is a male swan called?

5 What shape are the pupils in the eyes of a goat?

6 Which island is separated from mainland Britain by the Menai Straits?

7 An earthworm has no eyes – true or false?

Jackpot

The first factory-made cigarettes were sold in which year – 1856, 1876 or 1906?

✳Among those to have claimed to have encountered the ship in question was the future King George V, who was one of thirteen people to see the vessel during a voyage off the coast of Australia in 1880. Later that same day the sailor who had first sighted the vessel fell from a mast and was reportedly 'smashed to atoms'.

Quiz 8

Round 1: Pot Luck

1 How many squares does a chessboard have?

2 The equator does not go through India – true or false?

3 What was nicknamed a 'bone shaker'?

4 The Kaiser Chiefs are from which British city?

5 What is the sirocco – a dry wind, an ocean current or a thick mist?

6 Rikki-Tikki-Tavi, created by writer Rudyard Kipling, is what kind of animal?

7 Which disease killed 20 million elm trees in the UK?

Round 2: Pirates

1 By what name was Edward Teach better known?

2 What was the name of the one-legged pirate in *Treasure Island*?

3 Who played Captain Jack Sparrow in *Pirates of the Caribbean*?

4 What name is commonly given to the pirate skull and crossbones flag?

5 In the pirate song, how many men were there 'on a dead man's chest'?

6 What was a doubloon?

7 In J. M. Barrie's *Peter Pan*, how did Captain Hook lose his hand?

Half-time teaser

For an extra point, who can touch their toes without bending their knees?

Round 3: Family Matters

1 Babies have more bones than adults – true or false?

2 Who were the parents of Cain and Abel?

3 Which unfortunate family live next door to the Simpsons in the cartoon series?

4 Which character in Greek tragedy unknowingly killed his father and married his mother?

5 If I am your mother's sister, what relation am I to you?

6 Which family member was the subject of James Whistler's painting *Arrangement in Grey and Black*?

7 How were Queen Victoria and her husband Prince Albert related?

Round 4: Pot Luck

1 Who has four nephews called Pipeye, Peepeye, Pupeye and Poopeye?

2 Where do plants get nitrogen from – the air, soil or water?

3 Where might you view the Horseshoe Falls and the Rainbow Falls?

4 Who has had more number one hit songs in the UK – Michael Jackson, Madonna or Cliff Richard?

5 What is a natterjack – a snake, an ape or a toad?

6 What is measured on the Mohs scale?

7 What nationality was William Tell?

Jackpot

How many years will the average person spend eating during their lifetime – one year, five years or ten years?

⁎This character was actually inspired by a real person, a writer called William Henley, who had a big red beard and a crutch as well as a loud laugh and a lively character, although interestingly real-life pirate William Dampier apparently sailed with a one-legged cook of the same name, complete with eye patch.

Quiz 9

Round 1: Pot Luck

1 What was the colour of the horse made famous by novelist Anna Sewell?

2 What nationality is the fictional detective Maigret?

3 Which is the only US state that begins with the letter P?

4 What, in a German town, is the Rathaus?

5 Which one of the armed services has the rank of Petty Officer?

6 Which flower traditionally commemorates soldiers who have died in battle?

7 Which was the last battle to be fought on British soil?

Round 2: Nicknames

1 Which English king was nicknamed Lionheart?

2 In World War II, was the Stuka a dive-bomber, a tank or a gun?

3 Which city is sometimes nicknamed The Smoke?

4 Followers of which football club have the nickname Toffees? ✶

5 What nickname did supporters of King Charles I give his Parliamentarian enemies?

6 Which US city has the nickname Motown?

7 Which French king was known as The Sun King?

Half-time teaser

For an extra point, who can wiggle their ears?

Round 3: Foreign Parts

1 The names of all the continents end with the same letter they begin with – true or false?

2 Which is further west – Iran or Iraq?

3 Van Diemen's Land was the original name for which state – Canada, Cuba or Tasmania?

4 In which country is haggis a traditional dish?

5 The Iberian peninsula comprises which two countries?

6 What are the cowboys of Argentina called?

7 Which Pacific island is famous for hundreds of huge stone heads?

Round 4: Pot Luck

1 By what name is molten magma rock commonly known?

2 What did Colonel Thomas Blood try to steal in 1671?

3 The electric chair was invented by a dentist – true or false?

4 In tennis, what word describes a point in which the serve is not returned?

5 Which German battleship was destroyed by RAF bombs in a Norwegian fjord in 1944?

6 What kind of animal is a St Bernard?

7 What does a fletcher make?

Jackpot

How many hours a day does a koala spend sleeping – two, twelve or twenty-two?

✳The nickname referred to the toffees that were sold to early fans of the team from a nearby sweet shop by a woman known as Old Ma Bushell. Competition from the black-and-white striped mints made by the rival Mother Nobletts Toffee Shop encouraged Old Ma Bushell to seek permission to sell toffees inside the club's ground.

Quiz 10

Round 1: Pot Luck

1 What is the Richter scale used to measure?

2 What is the name of Postman Pat's cat?

3 Which of the following writers was female – Thomas Hardy, George Eliot or Daniel Defoe?

4 In which country was the Battle of the Boyne fought?

5 In which Hanna-Barbera cartoon did Officer Charlie Dibble appear?

6 Which British cathedral boasts a famous bronze of St Michael defeating the Devil?

7 What is the nickname of Manchester United?

Round 2: Gods and Goddesses

1 Where were the gods of ancient Greece said to live?

2 Who was the chief god in Norse mythology?

3 Which is the only planet in the solar system not named after a classical god?

4 What kind of building often has an upper area known as 'the gods'?

5 The Indian god Ganesh is usually depicted with the head of which animal?

6 After whom was Thursday named?

7 Who was the Roman god of war?

Half-time teaser

For an extra point, who (in ten seconds) can think of a (real) word with the most letters?

Round 3: Monsters

1 In Greek mythology, who killed the Minotaur?

2 Which monster made his first appearance in a Japanese film in 1954?

3 How did the mythological monster called the basilisk kill its victims?

4 What is the name of the hostile aliens in *Captain Scarlet*?

5 Which Scottish lake is world-famous for its monster?

6 By what other name is the yeti of the Himalayas known?✳

7 Which novels featured the brutish Orcs?

Round 4: Pot Luck

1 In which country is the Taj Mahal located?

2 What is the colour of the gemstone known as jet?

3 On which date is Hallowe'en celebrated?

4 In which country is the shekel the unit of currency?

5 What is the Old Man of Hoy – a rock stack in the Orkneys, an ancient Chinese philosopher or a disgusting old Irishman?

6 On which continent is the volcano Mount Erebus?

7 Alice Springs is a town in which country?

Jackpot

How many times did Michael Schumacher win the Formula One championship – five, seven or nine?

✳'Yeh-the' means 'the thing' in the Sherpa language.

Quiz 11

Round 1: Pot Luck

1 What do moles eat?

2 Which of the following sports does not involve balls – badminton, bowls or rugby?

3 To whom does Pikachu belong in *Pokemon*?

4 Who is the only footballer to have been voted BBC Personality of the Year since 2000?

5 Which battle took place on Senlac Hill?

6 In what kind of building do devout Jews worship?

7 Only female ducks quack – true or false?

Round 2: Rogues Gallery

1 Which criminal had a horse called Black Bess?

2 From which direction did the last surviving wicked witch of *The Wizard of Oz* come?

3 Lord Voldemort is the arch-enemy of which modern fictional character?

4 Professor Moriarty plunged over the Reichenbach Falls with which celebrated detective?

5 Soldiers of which Scottish clan carried out the massacre at Glencoe in 1691?

6 The Green Goblin is the sworn enemy of which superhero?

7 Which breed of supernatural creatures is often blamed when engines and other devices fail to work properly? ✳

Half-time teaser

For an extra point, who can do the best Scottish accent?

Round 3: Colours

1 What colour are holly berries?

2 Alongside red and white, which is the third colour on the Welsh flag?

3 Is a yellowhammer a kind of shark, a tiny yellow flower or a small bird?

4 Who is the only person to have sold more copies of one of their songs
   globally than Bing Crosby's 'White Christmas'?

5 What colour is topaz?

6 In which US city is the White House?

7 What colour are the cars run by the Ferrari Formula One racing team?

Round 4: Pot Luck

1 What is the Pope's home called?

2 What is a pig's gruntle?

3 In which Italian city is the Bridge of Sighs?

4 Xerxes was ruler of which ancient country?

5 The death of which US rock and roll star is commemorated in the song
   'American Pie'?

6 What type of animal is a falabella?

7 What was the name of King Arthur's wizard?

Jackpot

How many people are there in an official tug of war team – six, eight
or twelve?

✴The origins of these creatures are relatively recent. They seem to have been an
invention of RAF mechanics serving in India in the 1930s, when they were blamed for a
variety of technical problems. The only way to placate them is apparently to lay an
empty bottle on the ground in the hope that the mischievous creatures will crawl inside.

Quiz 12

Round 1: Pot Luck

1 Who had friends called Tuck, Marian and Little John?

2 A chameleon's tongue is twice as long as its body – true or false?

3 What is the name of the patron saint of Wales?

4 In which ocean is the island of Madagascar?

5 What is the motto of the SAS (Special Air Service)?

6 Where was the German fleet scuttled in 1919?

7 What is the name of the donkey in *Winnie-the-Pooh*?

Round 2: North of the Border

1 What is Scotland's national flower?

2 Which is further south – Aberdeen, Glasgow or Edinburgh?

3 Where is the Scottish Grand National run?

4 Ben Nevis is part of which Scottish mountain range?

5 What was Gavin Maxwell's 1960 novel about the lives of two otters on the west coast of Scotland?

6 Which early people lived in Scotland – the Franks, the Picts or the Gauls?

7 Skye is located off the east or west coast of Scotland?

Half-time teaser

For the youngest member of each team: For an extra point, who can spell their first name backwards, without writing it down, without making a mistake?

Round 3: Lovely Grub

1 What might be served 'sunny side up'?

2 Which of the following is not a type of apple – golden delicious, pearmain or maraschino?

3 From which animal does venison come?

4 Which edible fruit was originally called the spiky pear?

5 According to the Bible, what food sent from heaven did the Israelites live on while escaping from Egypt?

6 What kind of creature tempted Adam and Eve to eat the forbidden fruit?

7 Potato crisps were invented by George Crum in which year – 1803, 1853 or 1903?

Round 4: Pot Luck

1 According to the proverb, what should you make while the sun shines?

2 What do the initials of Roald Dahl's BFG stand for?

3 Which country has a flag nicknamed 'Old Glory'?

4 Which is the hottest planet in the solar system?

5 Nell Gwyn was a girlfriend of which king of England?

6 Who was British prime minister before Gordon Brown?

7 Vera Lynn was famous as what – a pilot, a dancer or a singer?

Jackpot

How long would it take to walk to the Sun – 20 years, 200 years or 2000 years?

✻ The story goes that the plant in question became Scotland's national flower after it helped to alert the defenders of a Scottish castle of the presence of Viking raiders after one of the attackers stepped on it.

Quiz 13

Round 1: Pot Luck

1 What kind of animal is Stuart Little?

2 Long before it became a heel, what was a stiletto?

3 Which English monarch was famous for not being amused? ✶

4 Which English county has its administrative headquarters at Aylesbury?

5 How many times have England appeared in the final of football's European Championship?

6 In which modern country is the region known as Transylvania?

7 What shopping innovation was introduced in an Oklahoma supermarket in June 1937?

Round 2: Cities of the World

1 Where in Italy might one see a gondola?

2 In which US state is the city of San Francisco?

3 What is the modern name of Constantinople?

4 Which US city is home to the Redskins NFL football team?

5 Which English city was known to the Romans as Verulamium?

6 The three largest cities in South America are São Paulo, Buenos Aires and which other?

7 In which city is the Aston Villa football team based?

Half-time teaser

For an extra point, who can burp the loudest?

Round 3: Back to School

1 Which house at Hogwarts School of Wizardry does Hermione Granger belong to?

2 What is the school in the Charles Dickens novel *Nicholas Nickleby*?

3 Who wrote *The School for Scandal*?

4 Who are the gang of riotous schoolchildren whose escapades have long been a feature of the *Beano* comic?

5 What kind of school starred Jack Black in 2003?

6 Which fictional schoolboy was created by Frank Richards?

7 Who had a fearsome headteacher called Mrs Trunchbull?

Round 4: Pot Luck

1 What is the highest point in Africa?

2 Dwarfs, red giants and white dwarfs are forms of what?

3 In which year was the Channel Tunnel opened – 1994, 1996 or 1998?

4 Who kill the most deer each year – hunters or drivers?

5 Who wrote *Water Music* for George I?

6 Which poet had the first names Percy Bysshe?

7 Which indoor sport is sometimes called ping-pong?

Jackpot

When were plus and minus signs first used in mathematics – the sixteenth, the seventeenth or the eighteenth century?

*Whether or not the person in question actually said it is a subject of debate. The most common suggestion is that it was first said after someone else told a rude joke that offended the ladies of the royal court.

Quiz 14

Round 1: Pot Luck

1 In the nursery rhyme, who took the kettle off after Polly had put it on?

2 Which English city had the Viking name Jorvik?

3 According to the proverb, all roads lead to where?

4 In which US state are the Everglades?

5 Charcoal is partly burnt what?

6 If something is described as stupendous what is it – impressive, stupid or stewed?

7 On which river does Liverpool stand?

Round 2: Great Explorers

1 Which country is said to have been named after explorer Amerigo Vespucci?

2 On which island was Captain Cook murdered – Hawaii, Pitcairn Island or the Isle of Wight?

3 Burke and Wills were pioneer explorers of which country?

4 Which explorer was Henry Stanley sent to Africa in 1871 to locate?

5 Which US spacecraft landed the first men on the moon?

6 Who discovered a strange new world after following a white rabbit down a rabbit hole?

7 Which Portuguese explorer died while heading the first voyage round the world?

Half-time teaser

For an extra point, who can touch their chin with the tip of their tongue?

Round 3: Yuletide Yak

1 Which plant used in Christmas decorations was sacred to Druids?

2 Which pantomime features Widow Twankey? ⭒

3 Father Christmas is sometimes identified by which saint's name?

4 Christmas crackers were invented in which year – 1747, 1847 or 1947?

5 Which of the following is not one of Father Christmas's reindeer – Blitzen, Lancer or Comet?

6 On what date is Boxing Day celebrated?

7 What did Harry Potter receive as a present at his first Christmas at Hogwarts?

Round 4: Pot Luck

1 The 14 most venomous snakes in the world live in which continent?

2 Dolphins sleep with one eye open – true or false?

3 Which county cricket team play at the Oval?

4 Which is the only kind of rock that can float in water?

5 How many golfballs are there on the moon – three, one or none?

6 What was the name of the amphitheatre in which the gladiators fought in Rome?

7 Great Britain comprises how many countries?

Jackpot

How many keys do most modern pianos have – sixty-eight, seventy-eight or eighty-eight?

⭒ The pantomime in question was first performed in the eighteenth century, when high society was gripped by enthusiasm for all things Chinese. Widow Twankey's odd name was actually a reference to the popular Tuon Ky brand of tea, shipped from China.

Quiz 15

Round 1: Pot Luck

1 Which day of the week comes first alphabetically?

2 What does a thermometer measure?

3 What kind of animal is a bobolink?

4 Shelbyville is a neighbouring town in which television cartoon series?

5 In which English county is the city of Carlisle?

6 The Rocky Mountains run down the eastern or the western side of the USA?

7 What would one do with Esperanto – drink it, speak it or play it?

Round 2: Wonderful Words

1 What does a conchologist collect?

2 If someone is described as star-crossed, are they lucky, unlucky or bad-tempered?

3 What is the plural of 'ox'?

4 What is the opposite of 'regular'?

5 What is graphology the study of?

6 What is a ballista – a drum, a hat or a catapult?

7 How many s's are there in 'necessary'?

Half-time teaser

For an extra point, who can stare at the person opposite the longest without blinking?

Round 3: Getting About

1 A rickshaw has how many wheels – four, two or none?

2 Which country has a high-speed train called the TGV?

3 Traffic lights were invented before the motor car – true or false? ✳

4 In the USA, what kind of vehicle is a Greyhound?

5 What early bicycle had a huge front wheel and a tiny back wheel?

6 The Orient Express connected Paris with which other city?

7 The world's first underground railway line was built in which city?

Round 4: Pot Luck

1 What is a young deer called?

2 During which month is Burns Night celebrated in Scotland?

3 In which country are Sinhalese and Tamil the national languages?

4 A Van-patterned cat has colour only on which parts of its body?

5 Which country is famous for its fjords?

6 Which mythical continent is said to have vanished beneath the waves of the Atlantic Ocean thousands of years ago?

7 Apes are kept in an apiary – true or false?

Jackpot

How many minutes does it take the average person to fall asleep – two, seven or ten?

✳ The first set of traffic lights, run on gas, were installed outside the Houses of Parliament in Westminster. Unfortunately, a month after being installed they blew up, injuring a policeman.

Quiz 16

Round 1: Pot Luck

1 What is a glacier largely made of?

2 Which country lies to the immediate west of Argentina?

3 Who spent his childhood in Smallville, USA?

4 What colours do Manchester City play in?

5 The rock band Franz Ferdinand come from which British city?

6 What lives in an eyrie?

7 If something is gargantuan, is it well-guarded, talkative or huge?

Round 2: Fabulous Firsts

1 What type of creature was the first living thing from Earth to go into space?

2 In 1927 Charles Lindbergh made the first solo crossing by air of which body of water?

3 What was first discovered by Watson and Crick in 1953?

4 What is the most popular first name in the world – Bill, Ali or Muhammad?

5 Where did Roger Bannister run the first four-minute mile – Oxford, Edinburgh or Manchester?

6 Who was the first British monarch to make an official visit to the USA?

7 Who was the first US president to eat ice cream?

Half-time teaser

For an extra point, who can hold their breath the longest?

Round 3: Out of Africa

1 Indian elephants have bigger ears than African elephants – true or false?

2 The springbok is the emblem of which African country?

3 Which sea separates Africa from Asia?

4 How many countries are there in Africa – thirty-three, forty-three or fifty-three?

5 Which of the following are not native to Africa – buffaloes, tigers or cheetahs?

6 What is the modern name of what used to be Zaire?

7 The defeat of British forces at Spion Kop in 1900 was an engagement in which war?

Round 4: Pot Luck

1 Which fictional character is said to have been inspired in part by the historical ruler Vlad the Impaler?✳

2 How many minutes are there in four and a half hours?

3 Where in the USA is the Dodgers baseball team based?

4 Where is the kimono a traditional form of dress?

5 Which fruit comes in Jaffa, clementine and mandarin varieties?

6 What nationality was the artist Salvador Dali?

7 By what name were the feared mounted fighters from the steppes of southern Russia known?

Jackpot

How many feathers does the average canary have – 1200, 2200 or 4400?

✳ In contrast to the modern view of Vlad the Impaler as an evil butcher who liked to execute his victims by impaling them on stakes, he was celebrated in his own time as a steadfast defender of Christianity against the threat posed by the Ottoman Empire.

Quiz 17

Round 1: Pot Luck

1 Which Carthaginian general crossed the Alps with elephants to attack Rome?

2 In the Mr Men books, what colour is Mr Tickle?

3 What percentage of the Earth's surface is water – 50 per cent, 70 per cent or 90 per cent?

4 Which art gallery stands on the north side of Trafalgar Square?

5 Most moths lack a mouth – true or false?

6 The word dressage is associated with what – horses, high fashion or ballet?

7 In which country was the first Disneyland resort in Asia opened?

Round 2: Dog Treats

1 Which breed of dog comes in border, bull and silky varieties?

2 In which children's classic is the family pet dog called Nana?

3 Which breed of dog is traditionally used to pull sleds?

4 What is unusual about the basenji breed of dog?

5 What is Tintin's dog called?

6 What is the most popular name for a dog in Britain?

7 What is the name of the dog in the *Peanuts* cartoons?

Half-time teaser

For an extra point, who can write their name best with the wrong hand (not the hand they normally write with)?

Round 3: Snakes and Reptiles

1 Which saint is said to have rid Ireland of its snakes? *

2 Which snake holds the record for the longest snake ever recorded?

3 Which physical feature do snakes share with hummingbirds?

4 The adder is Britain's only native venomous snake – true or false?

5 In Greek mythology, which one of the Gorgons had snakes for hair?

6 Which is the only continent that has no reptiles?

7 Some lizards produce venom – true or false?

Round 4: Pot Luck

1 In advertising, what is recommended 'for hands that do dishes'?

2 In the Uncle Remus stories, who got stuck to a Tar Baby?

3 In which country is Lake Como?

4 Acorns grow on which kind of tree?

5 Which one of these teams has not won the FA Cup since 2000 – Liverpool, Manchester United or Everton?

6 A killer whale is a member of the dolphin family – true or false?

7 What kind of instruments was Stradivarius famous for making?

Jackpot

In which year was the skateboard invented – 1858, 1938 or 1958?

*In fact, Ireland has not had snakes at any time since the last Ice Age. One suggestion is that the link with the saint in question may have its roots in the serpent symbolism of the Druids.

Quiz 18

Round 1: Pot Luck

1 Which sport is played with a shuttlecock?

2 In the Harry Potter books who has a pet called Fluffy?

3 Which bay lies off northern Spain and south-western France?

4 What was the name of the Venetian explorer who opened up trading contact with China?

5 In which sport do players stand at an oche (pronounced 'okky')?

6 Which two US states share no borders with other US states?

7 Which kind of animal comes in coral, garter and spitting varieties?

Round 2: Best of Britain

1 Which county is Norwich in?

2 Which television soap opera is set in Chester?

3 In which county is Stonehenge?

4 In which part of Britain does the average person spend the most on chocolate?

5 Which ancient earthwork roughly marks the border between Wales and England?

6 Which river is the longest – the Avon, the Severn or the Thames?

7 Where is Arthur's Seat?

Half-time teaser

For an extra point, who can list the most pantomimes?

Round 3: Flying High

1 The longest recorded flight achieved by a chicken lasted six, thirteen or twenty-three seconds?

2 The airline El Al is based in which country?

3 What name is commonly given to the automatic pilot on an aircraft?

4 What is the name given to the official aircraft assigned to the president of the USA?

5 The Zero fighter-bomber was used by which nation in World War II?

6 The 747 and 777 are successful aircraft produced by which manufacturer?

7 Which aeroplane came into service in 1976 and flew its last flight in 2003?

Round 4: Pot Luck

1 Cuban is the official language of Cuba – true or false?

2 What was the nickname of General Erwin Rommel?

3 What is a russophobic person afraid of?

4 Which British coin has a crowned thistle on it?

5 What does a carnivore eat?

6 At which sport did Lance Armstrong enjoy outstanding success?

7 Slugs have one, four or seven noses? ✶

Jackpot

How many times does a whale's heart beat per minute – nine, nineteen or ninety-nine times?

✶ Slugs belong to the group of animals called gastropods. The term 'gastropod' itself means 'belly feet', referring to how slugs move about.

Quiz 19

Round 1: Pot Luck

1 How many sides does a heptagon have?

2 Which country did the UK fight to regain control of the Falkland Islands in 1982?

3 Which two species did scientists crossbreed to produce a geep in 1982?

4 What takes the place of a ball in ice hockey?

5 Who wrote *My Family and Other Animals?*

6 How did Joan of Arc die – was she beheaded, hanged or burned at the stake?

7 Who plays Harry Potter in the films of the adventure stories by J. K. Rowling?

Round 2: Fairy Tales

1 Which fairytale character is forced to do the housework by her wicked stepmother?

2 Which film was advertised with the slogan 'The greatest fairy tale never told'?

3 Where do the Seven Dwarfs work?

4 Which brother and sister became prisoners in a gingerbread house?

5 Which Hans Christian Andersen character has a statue in Copenhagen harbour?

6 How did the prince manage to get to Rapunzel when she was imprisoned in a high doorless tower?

7 In which fairy tale is the beautiful Belle forced to go and live with a hideous monster?

Half-time teaser

For an extra point, can you whistle the *Blue Peter* theme tune?

Round 3: Indoor Games

1 How many prawns are there in a game of chess?

2 Which of the following is not one of the murder weapons in Cluedo – a rope, an axe or a candlestick?

3 What colour cards are used for history questions in the board game Trivial Pursuit?

4 How many balls are used in a game of snooker – eighteen, twenty-one or twenty-two?

5 Which is the only king without a moustache in a standard set of playing cards?

6 How many pieces does each player have in a game of draughts?

7 How many knights are there in a game of chess?

Round 4: Pot Luck

1 Which variety of pasta comes in long flat ribbons?

2 What kind of animal is measured in hands?

3 Which Great Dane kept company with Fred, Velma, Shaggy and Daphne? *

4 Who had a servant called Friday?

5 Which football team has the nickname The Blades?

6 Who led the Iceni in revolt against the Romans in 122 AD?

7 What is jujitsu – a Japanese food, a shaking disease spread by mosquitoes or a form of unarmed self-defence?

Jackpot

Cockroaches fart on average every fifteen, thirty or sixty minutes?

* When the series in question was first planned the original cast was to be Geoff, Mike, Kelly, Linda and W.W., together with their dog (either a Great Dane or a shaggy sheepdog) called Too Much.

Quiz 20

Round 1: Pot Luck

1 Which is the Eternal City?

2 How many lines are there in a limerick?

3 Which are the only birds that can fly backwards?

4 In which sport was a player nicknamed the Black Pearl a star?

5 What is celebrated in the UK on the fourth Sunday of Lent?

6 The Atlantic Ocean is saltier than the Pacific Ocean – true or false?

7 In *Toy Story 2*, what is the name of the evil emperor who threatens Woody and Buzz?

Round 2: Pick of the Pops

1 What is Geri Halliwell's name as one of the Spice Girls?

2 Which James was an officer in the Life Guards before releasing a 'beautiful' number one?

3 Billie Joe Armstrong is lead singer with which top US rock band?

4 Whose 2008 single 'Touch my body' made her second only to the Beatles in terms of US number ones?

5 With which song did Abba win the 1974 Eurovision Song Contest?

6 As what pop group did Natalie Appleton, Nicole Appleton, Melanie Blatt and Shaznay Lewis become well-known?

7 Which pop singer, usually known by her first name, has the second and third names Giselle Knowles?

Half-time teaser

For the youngest member of each team: For an extra point, who can name the most breakfast cereals?

Round 3: Disasters

1 Who built the Ark to survive the Great Flood described in the Bible?

2 What was the name given to the plague that wiped out a third of Europe's population in the fourteenth century?

3 Which volcano in Washington state erupted unexpectedly in 1980, causing widespread damage?

4 What disastrous fate befell Peter Rabbit's father?

5 What was the name of the Russian nuclear plant that suffered a disastrous failure in 1986?

6 The city of San Francisco was destroyed in 1906 by an earthquake along which fault?

7 Which volcano destroyed Pompeii in 79 AD?

Round 4: Pot Luck

1 What name is given to an otters' den?

2 Who ascended the English throne in 1837?

3 What kind of sport happens in a velodrome?

4 Which Roman emperor competed in the Olympic Games? *

5 What is the name of the family in *The Sound of Music*?

6 If something is described as 'ritzy', is it cheap, luxurious or stupid?

7 Tripoli is the capital of which African country?

Jackpot

How high can a flea jump – 3 centimetres, 30 centimetres or 300 centimetres?

*Among the events he took part in was the chariot race, of which he was declared the winner. This was despite the fact that he had actually fallen out of his chariot during the race.

Quiz 21

Round 1: Pot Luck

1 Who conducts his business from the Oval Office?

2 What is the last letter of the ancient Greek alphabet?

3 Which three colours appear on the Italian flag?

4 What kind of foodstuff is a cantaloupe?

5 Which warriors sailed the seas in longships?

6 Which martial art has a name that translates as 'empty hand'?

7 From whom did the USA buy Louisiana in 1803?

Round 2: Heavens Above

1 Which planet is nicknamed the Red Planet?

2 What was the name of the world's first artificial space satellite?

3 What first did Helen Sharman achieve in 1991?

4 Cirrus and cumulonimbus are types of what?

5 Which is the Land of the Long White Cloud?

6 Which is the largest planet in the solar system?

7 How long does it take the Sun's rays to reach Earth – eight seconds, eight minutes or eight hours?

Half-time teaser

For an extra point, who can be first to spot something triangular?

Round 3: Cartoon Capers

1 Which Disney animated film has a central character called Simba?

2 Which television cartoon series takes place in New New York?✳

3 In Disney's *Snow White*, which was the only one of the Seven Dwarfs to lack a beard?

4 Which cartoon rabbit was framed alongside human actors in a popular 1988 film?

5 Which Disney cartoon features three kittens called Marie, Berlioz and Toulouse?

6 Which cartoon character has the catchphrase 'Ssssh! Be vewwy, vewwy quiet. I'm hunting wabbits!'?

7 What is the name of the rabbit who becomes Bambi's best friend?

Round 4: Pot Luck

1 Who performed twelve mythological labours?

2 How many sides does an octagon have?

3 In the zodiac, what is the symbol for Taurus?

4 How many years pass between each Olympic Games?

5 A mandolin is a type of orange, a musical instrument or a Chinese official?

6 Who sang the James Bond theme song 'Diamonds are forever'?

7 What is the Sport of Kings?

Jackpot

In which year did the UK return Hong Kong to Chinese control – 1992, 1997 or 2000?

✳New York itself was not named directly after the city of York, but was named instead in honour of James Stuart, Duke of York, who in due course was crowned king of England as James II.

Quiz 22

Round 1: Pot Luck

1 What is the capital of Cuba?

2 What does the Tin Man seek in *The Wizard of Oz*?

3 Which British king gave up his throne in 1936?

4 Rugby League teams have eleven, thirteen or fifteen players?

5 Who won the award for Best Male Solo Artist at the Brit awards four times between 1999 and 2003?

6 Which part of the eye expands when a person looks at something pleasing?

7 Which British monarch was nicknamed 'Farmer George'?

Round 2: The Land of the Free

1 Which US state is known as The Lone Star State?

2 Who of the following does not appear among the presidents carved into Mount Rushmore – Washington, Jefferson, Lincoln or Truman?

3 What is the British equivalent of what Americans call a faucet?

4 The Niagara Falls on the US–Canada border have never frozen solid – true or false?

5 In which city is the Golden Gate Bridge?

6 Which US state is home to the Cajun culture – New Mexico, Louisiana or Florida?

7 For what purpose did the US inventor Thomas Alva Edison popularise the word 'hello'? ✳

Half-time teaser

For an extra point, who can think up the most words that rhyme with 'catch'?

Round 3: Bad Behaviour

1 Who might be killed in an act of regicide?

2 What does 'asbo' stand for?

3 Which Australian outlaw was famous for wearing home-made armour?

4 James Earl Ray was arrested in 1968 for assassinating which well-known figure?

5 Which plot planned the murder of James I in 1605?

6 If a person is guilty of 'twocking', what are they guilty of?

7 It is impossible for a crocodile to stick its tongue out – true or false?

Round 4: Pot Luck

1 Which children's novel describes the adventures of Charlie Bucket?

2 What is a bandicoot – a ratlike marsupial, a bird or a small antelope?

3 In which part of the world are there the most redheads?

4 Which organisation was founded by William Booth in 1865?

5 What was the magic phrase Ali Baba uttered to open the cave of the Forty Thieves?

6 Which war provided the setting for *All Quiet on the Western Front*?

7 What is a Venus Flytrap – a fly swatter, a car radiator grille or a plant?

Jackpot

The Antarctica contains what percentage of the world's fresh water – 50 per cent, 75 per cent or 90 per cent?

＊Edison is sometimes credited with actually inventing the word, although records exist of its use as early as 1826. It may have started life as a contraction of 'whole be thou' or else have developed from the greeting 'Hail, Thou', as recorded in the Bible.

Quiz 23

Round 1: Pot Luck

1 In 'Hickory Dickory Dock', what ran up the clock?

2 The *Venus de Milo* is what – a sort of hat, a musical instrument or a statue?

3 What is the most common reason given by children for not doing their homework?

4 According to the British prime minister Harold Macmillan, you've never had it so – what?

5 Under which sign of the zodiac does the year end on 31 December?

6 Which is the most frequently used letter in the English alphabet?

7 Checkpoint Charlie was a crossing point in which notorious barrier?

Round 2: Art and Artists

1 Who painted *The Hay Wain*?

2 George Stubbs was famous for painting which kind of animals?

3 By what name is the Leonardo da Vinci painting *La Gioconda* also known?

4 Which artist's best-known works included paintings of soup cans?

5 Vincent Van Gogh did not sell a single painting during his lifetime – true or false?

6 Whose admired paintings included *The Night Watch*?

7 In which European city is the Prado museum and art gallery?

Half-time teaser

For an extra point, who can draw the best face?

Round 3: Wildlife

1 Which breed of dog comes in Irish water, Tibetan and Welsh springer varieties?

2 A cross between a male lion and a female tiger produces a liger, but what do you get if you cross a male tiger with a female lion?

3 A Camberwell beauty is what – a small plant, a fish or a butterfly?

4 What kind of leaves do koala bears eat?

5 A leveret is a young form of which animal?

6 Which one of these is not an insect – a butterfly, an ant or a spider?

7 Giraffes cannot swim – true or false?

Round 4: Pot Luck

1 What was the language of the Romans?

2 Which car manufacturer makes the Boxster and the Carrera?

3 Which football team has the nickname Pompey?

4 How many pieces of silver did Judas get for betraying Christ?

5 Which ocean current carries warm water from the Caribbean towards Europe?

6 Which was William Shakespeare's home county?✳

7 Which of the following sports does not take place on ice or snow – curling, hurling or tobogganing?

Jackpot

How many eggs will the average hen lay in a year – 127, 227 or 327?

✳Various foreign scholars have tried to claim Shakespeare for their own nations. One Italian professor argued that he was born not in Stratford but in Messina, while several Arabic scholars have insisted he was Arabic and that he should properly be referred to as Sheikh al-Subair.

Quiz 24

Round 1: Pot Luck

1 The Pyrenees divide France from which country?

2 Which mythological hero set sail in the *Argo*?

3 Which is further south – Northampton or Northumberland?

4 Who won the boxing match known as the 'Thrilla in Manila'?

5 In which city was there an Easter Rising in 1916?

6 What is a ragout – a hairy ape, a stew or an Indian temple?

7 Which prison is guarded by the ghostly Dementors in the Harry Potter books of J. K. Rowling?

Round 2: Weatherwise

1 According to the proverb, every cloud has what?

2 The largest hailstone ever recorded was as large as a cricket ball, a football or a basketball?

3 Which US state has the most tornadoes – Florida, Texas or Virginia?

4 Are men or women more likely to be struck by lightning?

5 What coloured sky at night is a sign of good weather approaching?

6 When it rains heavily it is said to be raining cats and what?

7 What was the name of the hurricane that devastated New Orleans in 2005?

Half-time teaser

For an extra point, who can think of a first name with the most letters?

Round 3: Driving Issues

1 Which car manufacturer has a prancing black stallion as its badge? *

2 Which car company made the 'Tin Lizzie'?

3 What was Malcolm Campbell's record-breaking car called?

4 What make and model of car was Herbie?

5 What is the official road safety manual in the UK known as?

6 When Americans say 'hood', which part of a car are they referring to?

7 What does LPG stand for?

Round 4: Pot Luck

1 Which king founded England's first navy?

2 In Scottish football, who are the Dons?

3 What shape is a fossil ammonite?

4 At which ground does Warwickshire county cricket team play?

5 What material was used to construct the Statue of Liberty?

6 Which featherweight boxer has the nickname Prince?

7 The Boxer Rebellion took place in which country – India, Burma or China?

Jackpot

What is the official language of Sierra Leone – Portuguese, French or English?

* The prancing horse was originally the lucky badge of Count Francesco Baracca, a World War I Italian air ace who had it painted on the side of his aeroplane. Baracca's horse was red, but after he was killed in action other planes in his squadron bore a horse painted in mourning black, and thus it appeared on the cars.

Quiz 25

Round 1: Pot Luck

1 In which street did the Great Fire of London break out in 1666?

2 What colour is the cue ball in snooker?

3 In which country is the famous Valley of the Kings?

4 What is a female fox called?

5 Who invented dynamite?

6 What was Thomas Sheraton famous for making?

7 How old must a US president be?

Round 2: In with the New

1 New Year's Day is celebrated on which date?

2 What name is given to New Year celebrations in Scotland?

3 What ceremony involving a dark stranger brings luck to the household at New Year?

4 Who supposedly wrote the words of 'Auld Lang Syne'?

5 Which of these is not the name of a Chinese year – dog, eel or rat?

6 Where in New York do huge crowds gather to see in the New Year?

7 Babies born on New Year's Day share which star sign?

Half-time teaser

For an extra point, who can do the best impression of Gollum in *The Lord of the Rings*?

Round 3: Superheroes

1 What is the superhero identity of Peter Parker?

2 Which superhero carries a shield decorated in the style of the US flag?

3 What is Batman's real name?

4 Into which large green creature does Dr David Banner transform when angered?

5 The Fantastic Four comprise Mister Fantastic, the Invisible Woman, the Human Torch – and who else?

6 By what name is Oswald Cobblepot known in the *Batman* stories and films?

7 Which superhero has the real name Eric Twinge?

Round 4: Pot Luck

1 Ayers Rock is a notable geographical feature in which country?

2 Which king of England was the fattest – George III, George IV or Edward VIII?

3 How many stripes does a corporal usually have on his arm?

4 Which country has Amman as its capital?

5 What is one quarter of 48?

6 In which English county is the city of Exeter?

7 In which sport might a participant use the Fosbury Flop?

Jackpot

What percentage of all animals are insects – 50 per cent, 65 per cent or 80 per cent?

＊The person in question seems to have inherited his inventiveness from his parents: his father invented plywood.

Quiz 26

Round 1: Pot Luck

1 What is the name of the fantasy land where Peter Pan lives?

2 How many degrees are there in a semicircle?

3 When did the Japanese surrender in World War II – 1945, 1946 or 1947?

4 Which country includes among its rivers the Arno and the Po?

5 For which film did Russell Crowe win an Oscar as Maximus Decimus Meridius?

6 In which year was American football's Superbowl game first played – 1947, 1957 or 1967?

7 Who was the captain of the *Nautilus* in *Twenty Thousand Leagues Under the Sea*?

Round 2: Fictional Characters

1 Which fictional bear lives in Hundred Acre Wood?

2 In which film does James Bond confront the villain Scaramanga?

3 Who played Mrs Doubtfire in the 1993 film?

4 Who had best friends called Badger, Rat and Mole?

5 In which classic children's programme was Troy Tempest a central character? ✗

6 Which novel features the characters Cathy and Heathcliff?

7 What is the name of the nanny who arrives by umbrella to look after the Banks children?

Half-time teaser

For an extra point, who can be first to point to something coloured green?

Round 3: Science and Nature

1 What do seismologists study?

2 How many degrees make up a right angle?

3 Which of the continents has the least rain?

4 Which animal lives longer – a hippo or a rhino?

5 What was used to propel a sedan chair – horsepower, manpower or windpower?

6 Iron weighs more after it has rusted – true or false?

7 What is measured with a Geiger counter?

Round 4: Pot Luck

1 What is a Scout rally called?

2 What colour shirts are worn by Brazil's national football team?

3 On which day are pancakes traditionally eaten?

4 Which is the only bird that can swim but cannot fly?

5 What name is given by cricketers to an over in which no runs are scored?

6 What was the first full-length animated film made by Walt Disney?

7 What is a marmoset – a dog, a monkey or a rodent?

Jackpot

What is the record for the longest attack of hiccups – two years, twenty-three years or sixty-eight years?

✴ It is fairly well known that Troy Tempest was modelled on the US actor James Garner, but it is perhaps less widely known that the Aquaphibian king Titan was based on Laurence Olivier and that Marina was inspired by Brigitte Bardot.

Quiz 27

Round 1: Pot Luck

1 What is Superman's real name?

2 Who succeeded Ronald Reagan as US president?

3 What is the fantastic world in which the novels of Terry Pratchett take place?

4 Casablanca is a city in Algeria – true or false?

5 What is Ozzy Osbourne's first name – Don, John or Tom?

6 Of which instrument was Niccolò Paganini a master?

7 The bite of the tsetse fly spreads which disease?

Round 2: Islands

1 The island of Sicily lies off the southern tip of which nation?

2 Tresco is part of which island group?

3 On which island did the dodo live?

4 What is the name of the fictional island resort terrorised by a shark in *Jaws*?

5 Which series of video games is set on Angel Island?

6 The island of Brobdingnag features in which classic satirical book? ✳

7 Which organisation has its headquarters on Tracy Island?

Half-time teaser

For an extra point, who can whistle while breathing in?

Round 3: Young and Old

1 What is a young goose called?

2 What is the traditional way to tell the age of a horse?

3 Which of the existing buildings is older – Westminster Abbey or St Paul's Cathedral?

4 What is a young kangaroo called?

5 Who holds the record for being the oldest person to occupy the throne of England?

6 Jacobite leader Charles Edward Stuart was known as the Young – what?

7 What is a young whale called?

Round 4: Pot Luck

1 Cows can sleep standing up – true or false?

2 What is campanology the study of?

3 For whom does Hayley Mills mistake a fugitive on the family farm in the 1961 film *Whistle Down the Wind*?

4 In which sport do teams play chukkas lasting seven and a half minutes?

5 How long does it take the Earth to go round the Sun?

6 How many lanes are there in an Olympic swimming pool – eight, ten or twelve?

7 What, according to a recent survey, is the most popular sandwich filling among British schoolchildren?

Jackpot

Where did feta cheese originate – Italy, Turkey or Greece?

✳ Brobdingnag is remarkable for the huge size of its inhabitants, and the adjective Brobdingnagian is sometimes used to describe anything of enormous size. According to the author, the island of Brobdingnag, which is 6000 miles long and 3000 miles wide, is situated north-west of California.

Quiz 28

Round 1: Pot Luck

1 In which Disney cartoon film are Perdita and Pongo central characters?

2 What is the capital of Wales?

3 Identical twins have identical fingerprints – true or false?

4 Which poet wrote 'The Pied Piper of Hamelin'?

5 Who wrote the novels *Pride and Prejudice* and *Sense and Sensibility*?

6 What is William Wilberforce remembered for campaigning against?

7 What is a boomslang?

Round 2: Good Sports

1 In a tennis match, what is the score if both players are at deuce?

2 In which indoor sport was 'Crafty Cockney' Eric Bristow a champion?

3 Who was replaced as England's football manager by Fabio Capello in 2007?

4 How many people are there in a baseball team?

5 Nasser Hussain was captain of which cricket team – England, India or Pakistan?

6 What is the nickname of the Welsh national rugby team?

7 Wentworth in Surrey is associated primarily with which sport?

Half-time teaser

For an extra point, who can sing 'We wish you a merry Christmas' to the tune of 'Frère Jacques' best?

Round 3: High Society

1 How many kings of England have been called Edward?

2 Galahad, Lancelot and Perceval were all members of which noble organisation?

3 Who was the first of the House of Windsor to occupy the British throne?

4 What is the name of the royal palace in Edinburgh?

5 Who lives at the Elysée Palace in France?

6 Jacqueline Bouvier was married to which US president?

7 What is the official motto of British kings and queens?

Round 4: Pot Luck

1 At which bar does Homer Simpson drink?

2 Which queen ruled first – Elizabeth I or Mary I?

3 What did Ives McGaffey invent in 1868 to leave housework to suckers?

4 Brittany belongs to which country – Britain, Ireland or France?

5 What was the name of the island on which Nelson Mandela was imprisoned until 1990?

6 The airline Qantas is based in which country?

7 Which US president was nicknamed Honest Abe?

Jackpot

How long is a giraffe's tongue – 14 inches, 21 inches or 37 inches?

⋆The historical origins of the legend are unclear. It may have been inspired by the deaths of many children during the Black Death or another epidemic. Alternatively, it may be a reference to the Children's Crusade of 1212, when thousands of children died while marching to reclaim the Holy Land for Christianity.

Quiz 29

Round 1: Pot Luck

1 What is a hurricane in the Pacific called?

2 According to the proverb, you can't get what out of a stone?

3 What was the only thing left in Pandora's box after she opened it?

4 Which weapon was designed for the Dambusters by Barnes Wallis?

5 Lack of sleep will kill a person quicker than lack of food – true or false?

6 What building housed the Great Exhibition of 1851?

7 Who is the most recent British tennis player to have won a singles title at Wimbledon?

Round 2: Boys in Blue

1 What is the name of the headquarters of London's Metropolitan Police?

2 What is the name of the chief of police in *The Simpsons*?

3 What colour caps do members of the British military police wear?

4 What is the International Criminal Police Organisation otherwise known as?

5 What was the name of Inspector Morse's sidekick?

6 What is the name of the police station in the long-running television series *The Bill*?

7 What is a police van used to transport prisoners known as – a Black Maria, a Blue Meanie or a White Wagon?

Half-time teaser

For an extra point, who can think of the shortest word in which the letter A appears twice?

Round 3: Nursery Rhymes

1 What did Old Mother Hubbard go to her cupboard for?

2 Which nursery rhyme character went to Gloucester?

3 What did Georgie Porgie do when the boys came out to play?

4 Where was Little Boy Blue?

5 In the nursery rhyme, who marched his men to the top of the hill? ✶

6 Which nursery rhyme character lost her pocket?

7 Where did Mary's little lamb follow her to?

Round 4: Pot Luck

1 In the *Arabian Nights*, who stole the treasure of the Forty Thieves?

2 What kind of animal comes in hairstreak and meadow brown varieties?

3 Who led a mutiny against Captain Bligh on the *Bounty* in 1787?

4 Sea snakes are the most poisonous of all snakes – true or false?

5 By what name is singer Anna Mae Bullock better known?

6 After which legendary figure was Rome named?

7 In World War II, was the V-1 a tank, an aeroplane or a flying bomb?

Jackpot

When was Switzerland last at war – 1815, 1915 or 1945?

✶ The rhyme is thought to refer to a brief invasion of the Netherlands staged by British forces in 1793. The hill in the rhyme is probably that on which the town of Cassel stands in the middle of the otherwise flat Flanders countryside.

Quiz 30

Round 1: Pot Luck

1 What does a milliner make or sell?

2 Of which country is Prague the capital city?

3 Which drink is sometimes nicknamed 'Adam's ale'?

4 In which sport might you use a niblick?

5 During which battle did the Charge of the Light Brigade take place?

6 Which type of bird comes in chinstrap, macaroni and emperor varieties?

7 Which was the only part of his body in which the hero Achilles was vulnerable?

Round 2: Down Under

1 Motorists in Australia drive on the left – true or false?

2 Which of the following is not in Australia – Sydney, Brisbane or Wellington?

3 What colour shirts are worn by Australia's rugby union team?

4 On which ship did Captain Cook explore Australia and New Zealand?

5 Which of these animals are not native to Australia – koalas, wallabies or yaks?

6 How many stars are there on the Australian flag?

7 Which city is capital of Australia?

Half-time teaser

For an extra point, who can think of three car manufacturers beginning with M?

Round 3: First and Last

1 What is the first consonant in the English alphabet?

2 Which US state would come last in an alphabetical list?

3 Which country holds the record for coming last in the Eurovision Song Contest the most times?

4 Who, in 1961, became the first man in space?

5 Which famous composer had the first name Ludwig?

6 Who was the last wife of Henry VIII?

7 What is the last letter in 'tumble'?

Round 4: Pot Luck

1 With which cartoon character is the catchphrase 'Yabba-dabba-doo!' associated?

2 Elephants cannot jump – true or false?

3 What is ornithology the study of?

4 From which country did the USA buy Alaska in 1867?

5 William Hartnell was the first person to play which famous role on television?

6 Which biblical character spent three days and nights inside a whale?

7 To which species of fish does the central character in the 2003 film *Finding Nemo* belong?

Jackpot

What was Queen Victoria's first name – Alexandrina, Catherina or Myrtle?

⁎There are various reasons why motorists in some countries drive on the left, while others keep to the right. One factor was the width of the horse-drawn wagons formerly in use – in countries like America, where the wagons were wider and were pulled by pairs of horses, the driver rode a horse on the left-hand side and thus preferred to keep to the right to have a better view of the road ahead.

Quiz 31

Round 1: Pot Luck

1 What was Jack Sprat's wife unable to eat?

2 Burmese, Manx and Maine Coon are all varieties of what?

3 Which European city was blockaded by the Soviet Union in 1948?

4 Who was known as 'the Hanging Judge'?

5 From which show does the song 'Ding dong the witch is dead' come?

6 Which heavyweight boxer was nicknamed Iron Mike?

7 Which US president resigned as a result of the Watergate Affair?

Round 2: Vampires and Ghosts

1 Which vegetable is said to ward off vampires?

2 Who created the fictional vampire Dracula?

3 Who was the friendly ghost who starred in a 1995 feature film?

4 Who met his father's ghost at the start of a famous Shakespeare play?

5 What kind of ghost confines itself to moving things around and generally causing a nuisance?

6 Which region of Europe is supposedly Dracula's homeland?

7 What was the name of the vampire slayer played on television by Sarah Michelle Gellar from 1997 to 2003?

Half-time teaser

For an extra point, who can list most of the colours in the rainbow?

Round 3: Fashion

1 What, over the years, has come in A-line, maxi and ra-ra varieties?

2 Which item of clothing was named after an atoll in the Pacific Ocean?

3 Whereabouts on your clothing might you find the initials YKK?

4 Where might a man wear a goatee?

5 What name is given to the protective leather trousers worn by cowboys in the American West?

6 Which language gave us the word 'anorak'?

7 What kind of tweed cap with ear flaps did Sherlock Holmes wear?

Round 4: Pot Luck

1 Which can survive longer without water – a camel or a rat?

2 What innovation introduced to England by Sir John Harington in 1589 proved a great convenience?

3 What nationality was Pope John Paul II?

4 Who was the last Tudor monarch of England?

5 How many seconds are there in two and a half minutes?

6 What is the Japanese art of raising miniature trees known as?

7 What is the maximum number of points that a player can score with three darts?

Jackpot

In which year was the first episode of *Coronation Street* broadcast, 1950, 1960 or 1970?

✳ The sensitive question of whether the friendly ghost in question was actually dead was avoided in earlier television series by the explanation that he was a ghost because his parents were already ghosts when they married.

Quiz 32

Round 1: Pot Luck

1 Which nursery rhyme character spilled her curds and whey?

2 What comes in such varieties as canine, incisor and molar?

3 Which instrument did Sherlock Holmes play in his spare time?

4 By what score did England beat West Germany in the 1966 World Cup Final?

5 To which South American country does Easter Island belong?

6 What was the date upon which World War I ended?

7 In which city was the composer Mozart born – Paris, Berlin or Salzburg?

Round 2: Countries of the World

1 Which country is sometimes called the Emerald Isle?

2 What is the capital of Canada – Ottawa, Montreal or Vancouver?

3 Which country first granted women the right to vote – the UK, New Zealand or the USA?

4 Of which country is Valletta the capital city?

5 Which three countries share a border with Luxembourg?

6 Which country annually donates the Christmas tree erected in Trafalgar Square?

7 What is the modern name of Kampuchea?

Half-time teaser

For an extra point, who can blow the loudest raspberry?

Round 3: Radio and Television

1 Television comedians Barry and Paul Elliot are better known as what?

2 What is the name of the village in which the action of the radio series *The Archers* takes place? ✳

3 Len Goodman, Arlene Phillips, Bruno Tonioli and Craig Revel Horwood are the panel in which television talent show?

4 Which US television series featured investigators Mulder and Scully?

5 Which character in television's *Star Trek* had green blood (T positive)?

6 In which children's programme was Edwin Jones the Steam a character?

7 Who was the victim of allegedly racist comments made by Jade Goody in *Celebrity Big Brother* in 2007?

Round 4: Pot Luck

1 On which river does Vienna stand?

2 Who pulled pussy out of the well?

3 What kind of weapon fires a bolt?

4 By what name did movie star Marion Morrison become better known?

5 What is the maximum number of rounds possible in a boxing match?

6 Which city has a Wailing Wall?

7 Which New York City park claims the title of most visited urban park in the USA?

Jackpot

In which year were British troops rescued from Dunkirk – 1939, 1940 or 1941?

✳ When the programme was being researched the original writers gleaned material from real places and characters. The village itself shares several characteristics with the Worcestershire village of Inkberrow, whose picturesque Old Bull pub is often used for pictures of the fictional Bull.

Quiz 33

Round 1: Pot Luck

1 According to the proverb, a what and his money are soon parted?

2 How old was Adrian Mole when he wrote the first volume of his secret diary?

3 Which Tudor warship was raised near Portsmouth in 1982?

4 Which musical instrument is played by Eric Clapton, Jimmy Page and Pete Doherty?

5 What was the name of the elephant that was a chief attraction of P. T. Barnum's famous travelling circus?

6 Which country did Britain and France fight during the Crimean War?

7 What is the capital of Romania?

Round 2: Mountains and Molehills

1 What is the highest mountain in the Alps called?

2 What nationality was the surveyor after whom Mount Everest was named?

3 In which city would you find the Palatine Hill?

4 From which show does the song 'Climb every mountain' come?

5 Cape Town is overlooked by which mountain?

6 Which is the highest mountain in England?

7 Where is Henman Hill?

Half-time teaser

For an extra point, who can get closest to licking their own elbow?

Round 3: Partners

1 By what names are television presenters Richard McCourt and Dominic Wood better known?

2 Barney Rubble is whose best friend?

3 Who was Tweedledum's twin brother?

4 What were Stan and Ollie better known as?

5 Which of the following was not one of the Three Musketeers – Poncho, Athos or Aramis?

6 Who has a best friend called Boo-Boo?

7 With whom did Ginger Rogers have a successful dance partnership in the movies?

Round 4: Pot Luck

1 Which of these countries does not share a border with Afghanistan – Iran, Iraq or Pakistan?

2 Which artist cut off his left ear in 1888?✳

3 A starfish can turn its stomach inside out – true or false?

4 Which of these is not an island – Iona, Lindisfarne or Dunfermline?

5 Under what name were Action Man toy figures originally sold in the USA?

6 Which US city is home to the Yankees baseball team?

7 Which biblical leader was found as a baby in the rushes?

Jackpot

What percentage of people are left-handed – 11 per cent, 21 per cent or 31 per cent?

✳ Having cut off his ear, the artist in question carefully wrapped the severed ear in newspaper and sent it to a girlfriend, asking her to keep it safe.

Quiz 34

Round 1: Pot Luck

1 Which 2000 film told the story of a working-class lad's ambition to become a ballet dancer?

2 What does HB on a pencil stand for?

3 What is the name of the boy spy created by Anthony Horowitz?

4 From which country did Napoleon retreat in 1812?

5 Which one of the Beatles had the middle name Winston?

6 What is the principal ingredient of laverbread?

7 How many stars are there on the flag of New Zealand?

Round 2: The Body

1 Who blink more often – men or women?

2 Whereabouts in the body might one find a labyrinth?

3 What colour hair does Pippi Longstocking have?

4 Conjunctivitis affects which part of the body?

5 How many chambers does the human heart have – two, four or six?

6 Which nail on a person's hand grows the slowest?

7 What are a person's eyeteeth otherwise known as?

Half-time teaser

For an extra point, who can do the best impression of Elvis Presley?

Round 3: All at Sea

1 The Tasmanian Sea lies between Australia and which other country?

2 In Greek mythology, who fell into the sea after flying too close to the Sun?

3 Which disease formerly affected sailors lacking sufficient intake of vitamin C?

4 What kind of vehicle made its first Channel crossing in 1959?

5 What name is given to a sailor's flared trousers?

6 Who sailed round the world in the *Golden Hind*? *

7 The Skagerrak lies between which two countries?

Round 4: Pot Luck

1 Erinsborough is the setting for which television soap opera?

2 What is the symbol of the Republican Party in the USA?

3 What colour is the Northern Line on maps of the London Underground?

4 In which sport may a participant perform a triple salchow?

5 What animal did Pinocchio find himself turned into?

6 A sheet bend, a sheepshank and a bowline are all varieties of what?

7 Which television series featured Kermit the Frog and Miss Piggy?

Jackpot

In which year was the ballpoint pen invented – 1918, 1928 or 1938?

* Two replicas of the *Golden Hind* have been constructed in recent years. The original ship was allowed to rot away, although a fragment of it survives in the form of a chair made from its timbers, now preserved in the Ashmolean Museum, Oxford.

Quiz 35

Round 1: Pot Luck

1 Who was Anne Hathaway's husband?

2 Which country fought Rome in the Punic Wars?

3 Which facial feature does the Mona Lisa lack?

4 What kind of animal is a dunnock?

5 Which direction lies opposite to north-east?

6 In which sport do participants contest the Ascot Gold Cup?

7 In which country did Elizabeth II receive the news that she was queen?

Round 2: Beginnings

1 According to the Book of Genesis, what did God create on the first day?

2 Who began a famous diary on 1 January 1660?

3 Which book begins: 'Mr and Mrs Dursley, of number four Privet Drive, were proud to say that they were perfectly normal, thank you very much'?

4 Amazon.com was founded in which year – 1984, 1994 or 2004?

5 Chess was first played in India – true or false?

6 What officially begins each year on 22 or 23 September?

7 Which boy band were at number one in the UK charts on 1 January 2000 with the double-A side 'I have a dream/Seasons in the sun'?

Half-time teaser

For an extra point, who can hum the opening bars of Beethoven's *Fifth Symphony*?

Round 3: Little and Large

1 Who was nicknamed 'The Little Corporal'?

2 A whale egg is the largest egg in the animal kingdom – true or false?

3 What kind of animal is a chihuahua?

4 Which is the largest island in the Mediterranean – Crete, Cyprus or Sicily?

5 Who introduced the concept of 'Big Brother'?

6 The komodo is the largest of which family of animals?

7 Which animal has the largest eyes – camels, ostriches or giant squids?

Round 4: Pot Luck

1 Which day of the year is celebrated as Independence Day in the USA?

2 Only female mosquitoes bite – true or false?

3 What does a bibliophile collect?

4 Sean is an Irish equivalent of which first name?

5 How many musicians are there in a sextet?

6 What feature of a medieval castle appears on a 1p coin?

7 Which country was the first to have a female prime minister?

Jackpot

Who ruled first – Julius Caesar, Nero or Caligula?

✶ The famous diarist in question eventually gave up writing his diary because he was afraid it was destroying his eyesight. Modern doctors, however, are convinced it would probably have caused him no harm whatsoever.

Quiz 36

Round 1: Pot Luck

1 There are no polar bears in the Antarctic – true or false?

2 Which sport includes a butterfly event?

3 Who wrote *The Magic Flute*?

4 Which is the biggest country in Africa?

5 'Leopard' and 'panther' are different names for the same animal – true or false?

6 What grows from a follicle?

7 What condition is insulin used to treat?

Round 2: Catchphrases

1 Whose catchphrase is 'What's up doc?'?

2 Which Catherine Tate character isn't 'bovvered'?

3 From which television comedy comes the catchphrase 'I have a cunning plan'?

4 Whose catchphrases include 'Eat my shorts'?

5 Which movie actor made a catchphrase of his line 'You talkin' to me?'?

6 Which character had as his catchphrase 'To infinity and beyond'?

7 From which 1984 film came the catchphrase 'I'll be back'?

Half-time teaser

For the youngest member of each team: For an extra point, who can tell the funniest joke?

Round 3: On the Box

1 Television pictures are composed of just three colours, of which two are red and blue – what is the third?

2 In *Dr Who*, which evil beings come from the planet Skaro?

3 Who hosts the television archaeology series *Time Team*?

4 The television programme *Blue Peter* began in which year – 1948, 1958 or 1968?

5 Which war provided the setting for the television series *M✷A✷S✷H*?

6 Which popular TV series concerned the defence of a small coastal resort called Walmington-on-Sea?✷

7 In which city is the television series *Byker Grove* set?

Round 4: Pot Luck

1 What does a meteorologist study?

2 By what name was Thailand known until 1939?

3 Who designed the *Great Western*, the *Great Britain* and the *Great Eastern*?

4 Who wrote *Water Music* and *Music for the Royal Fireworks*?

5 Where might you find triangles, tubas and timpani?

6 Whereabouts in Europe is The Hague?

7 Who buried the treasure found at Sutton Hoo in Suffolk in 1939 – the Romans, the Anglo-Saxons or the Spanish?

Jackpot

When was the death penalty for murder abolished in Britain – 1959, 1965 or 1969?

✷Originally called Brightsea-on-Sea, the town is located on the south coast of England. Various clues, such as the cap badges worn by the cast and the fact that the police station noticeboard reads 'Kent Constabulary', suggest that Walmington-on-Sea is in Kent, although it is thought to be modelled on the Sussex resort of Bexhill-on-Sea. All the filming actually took place at Thetford in faraway inland Norfolk.

Quiz 37

Round 1: Pot Luck

1 What kind of animal lives in a sett?

2 How many balls do you need to play a game of snooker?

3 In which war was the Battle of Edgehill fought?

4 Where might one come across an arpeggio – in a piece of music, in a castle or in a sandwich?

5 What are the traditional soft leather shoes of Native Americans called?

6 How many hours are there in a week – 148, 168 or 188?

7 In which sport might a player wear plus-fours?

Round 2: Rivers

1 Which river does Rome stand on?

2 The Tay is the longest river in which country?

3 Which Indian river is sacred to Hindus?

4 In which field did River Phoenix establish a reputation – sport, rock music or the cinema?

5 Saudi Arabia has no rivers – true or false?

6 What is the English name for China's Huang He river, suggested by its colour?

7 Who topped the UK charts in 1978 with 'Rivers of Babylon'?

Half-time teaser

For an extra point, who can stick both their legs out horizontally and keep them up (unsupported) for the longest?

Round 3: What's in a Name

1 What is the most popular name for a pope – Paul, John or Nigel?

2 How many kings of England have been called Charles?

3 Which author invented the first name Wendy?✳

4 By what name was Ho Chi Minh city formerly known?

5 What were the supporters of Bonnie Prince Charlie called?

6 Enid Darrell-Waters became the world's most popular children's writer using what name?

7 By what name is Arthur Wellesley usually remembered?

Round 4: Pot Luck

1 What name is given to a group of lions?

2 Which actor provides the voice of Bob the Builder?

3 How many arms do starfish usually have?

4 In text messaging, what do the initials FWIW stand for?

5 The island of Madeira belongs to which country?

6 In which French city was Joan of Arc burned at the stake?

7 Superman is described as faster than a speeding bullet and stronger than what?

Jackpot

In which year did India become independent of Britain – 1927, 1947 or 1967?

✳ The name apparently came about through a young girl calling the author her 'fwendy-wendy'.

Quiz 38

Round 1: Pot Luck

1 Which country was ruled by the shoguns?

2 What colour are taxis in New York?

3 Is a Kerry Blue a type of cheese, a breed of dog or a shade of light blue?

4 What kind of crab shelters in the discarded shells of other animals?

5 What is an athlete's PB?

6 What was the first name of the character played by Julie Andrews in the film *The Sound of Music*?

7 What is the name of the small girl in the *Just William* books who threatens to scream and scream until she is sick?

Round 2: The Wild West

1 Which Wild West outlaw was shot by Bob Ford?

2 Who starred as Marshal Rooster Cogburn in the film *True Grit*?

3 By what name was William Cody better known?

4 What in the slang of the Wild West was Boot Hill?

5 Which is the odd one out – Colt, Smith and Wesson, Hoover?

6 In which musical do the Sharks oppose the Jets?

7 Westlife's first seven releases all reached number one – true or false?

Half-time teaser

For an extra point, who can do the best Irish accent?

Round 3: Drinks and Nibbles

1 A raisin is the dried form of which fruit?

2 Eating chocolate is dangerous for dogs – true or false?

3 What is Calvados brandy made from?

4 In Greek mythology, what was the name of the drink enjoyed by the gods on Mount Olympus?

5 Who supposedly remarked of the starving poor 'Let them eat cake'? ⋆

6 What is the main ingredient of a Molotov cocktail?

7 Which of the following is not a nut – macadamia, pecan or pretzel?

Round 4: Pot Luck

1 Which is the world's smallest continent?

2 In which religion are services led by a rabbi?

3 In television's *Thunderbirds*, by what name was Hiram Hackenbacker better known?

4 Which of the following is not a piece in chess – castle, knight, duke?

5 Robert Plant is the lead singer with which rock band?

6 LBJ were the initials of which US president?

7 Which pop star married Guy Ritchie in the year 2000?

Jackpot

How tall is Mount Everest to the nearest mile – 1 mile, 5 miles or 9 miles?

⋆The person in question almost certainly never said any such thing, though, according to the French philosopher Jean-Jacques Rousseau, Louis XIV's queen, Maria Theresa of Spain, once remarked of the starving poor 'If there be no bread, let them eat piecrust'.

Quiz 39

Round 1: Pot Luck

1 According to the proverb, what makes the heart grow fonder?

2 Who seized power in Cuba on 1 January 1959?

3 Which is the only metal that is liquid at room temperature?

4 Who is the patron saint of travellers?

5 What is palaeontology the study of?

6 How long does a boxing round last?

7 What does 'vociferous' mean – outspoken, poisonous or inflammable?

Round 2: Up, Up and Away

1 What was the name of the winged horse of Greek mythology?

2 What colour is an aeroplane's black box flight recorder?

3 What was the name of the space shuttle that exploded after take-off in 1986?

4 What is Sir Frank Whittle remembered for inventing?

5 Which German airship was destroyed by fire in 1937 at Lakehurst, New Jersey?

6 Where is the O'Hare airport?

7 Which is the only mammal that can properly fly?

Half-time teaser

For an extra point, in two minutes who can make the most words of two or more letters out of 'explainable'?

Round 3: Connections

1 What is the name of the canal that connects the Mediterranean with the Red Sea?

2 Which two countries share borders with the USA?

3 What was the mythological creature that was half man and half horse called?

4 Merrill, Jay and Donny were members of which 1970s pop group?

5 Which country would one travel through to get from Libya to Morocco?

6 By what bird-related nickname are the football clubs Newcastle United and Notts County linked?

7 Which two continents share a land border?

Round 4: Pot Luck

1 By what name was King Ethelred II known – the Unruly, the Unrealistic or the Unready?

2 A Persian Blue is a variety of what?

3 What is 20 per cent of 50?

4 When was the last time the host country won football's World Cup?

5 Which 1972 book by Richard Adams featured rabbits called Hazel and Bigwig?

6 A double axel is a move in which sport?

7 Alongside Tommy Lee Jones, who was the other Man in Black?

Jackpot

What kind of acid is there in a bee sting – sulphuric acid, formic acid or acetic acid?

✴The airship in question features on the cover of the first Led Zeppelin album. The band itself had adopted the name Led Zeppelin after drummer Keith Moon had prophesied that they would 'go down like a lead balloon'.

Quiz 40

Round 1: Pot Luck

1 Which Italian city is famous for a leaning tower?

2 Which is the fourth consonant to appear in the English alphabet?

3 Which is the largest of the US states?

4 A baby rat is called a kitten – true or false?

5 On which street do the characters of television's *Neighbours* live?

6 What was Jumanji in the 1995 film of the same name?

7 Which pair of ice-skaters won Olympic gold for Britain in 1984?

Round 2: Planet Earth

1 There is no land at the North Pole, only ice – true or false?

2 Which of the following countries does not include part of the Amazon rainforest – Brazil, Ecuador, Venezuela or Indonesia?

3 Who accompanied Sir Edmund Hillary to the top of Everest in 1953?

4 Where is Timbuktu – Africa, Australia or South America?

5 Which is the highest country in the world?

6 Which country would one travel through to get from India to Afghanistan?

7 Which of the following is not one of the seven seas – the North Atlantic, the Mediterranean or the Indian Ocean?

Half-time teaser

For an extra point, in two minutes, who can think of think of the most ways of adding two numbers together to make 11?

Round 3: Top of the Pops

1 Which rock band is Mick Jagger singer with?

2 Colonel Tom Parker served as manager of which famous pop star?

3 From which British city do the Arctic Monkeys come?

4 Who wrote the hit musical *Oklahoma!*?

5 Which instrument did jazz musician Fats Waller play?

6 What kind of hairstyle is Amy Winehouse well-known for?

7 Which rock group included in its line-up Johnny Rotten and Sid Vicious?

Round 4: Pot Luck

1 What is a VIP?

2 What is the collective noun for a group of porpoises?

3 In 'Sing a song of sixpence', how many blackbirds were baked in a pie?

4 Which motor-racing circuit has been home to the British Formula One Grand Prix since 1987?

5 An elver is a baby what?

6 Which English king died after being shot by an arrow while besieging a castle in France?

7 Neapolitan ice cream comes in which three colours?

Jackpot

What is the average number of sesame seeds on a McDonald's Big Mac bun – 178, 278 or 378?

✻ The famous photograph taken on the summit of Mount Everest is of Hillary's companion. There is no photograph of Hillary himself as his companion did not know how to operate the camera. The pair left chocolate and a cross on the summit as an offering to the mountain.

Quiz 41

Round 1: Pot Luck

1 Who became leader of the Conservative party in 2005?

2 Princess Tiger Lily is a character in which children's classic?

3 A monkey-puzzle is a game, a fish or a tree?

4 The equator goes through three South American countries – Ecuador, Colombia and which other?

5 Which British monarch was on the throne at the time of the American War of Independence?

6 According to the Old Testament, how did the priests of Joshua destroy the walls of Jericho?

7 Which animal is sometimes called an Orca?

Round 2: Popular Places

1 Benidorm is a resort in which country?

2 Which market town in south-west France has a shrine that attracts thousands of pilgrims seeking miraculous cures each year?

3 What was the mythical golden city sought by explorers and buccaneers in South America in the sixteenth century?

4 In which London building can visitors view Poets' Corner?

5 Which Nevada city is famous for its many casinos?

6 In which county are such tourist destinations as Exmoor, Ilfracombe and Torquay?

7 Which is the most visited theme park in the UK?

Half-time teaser

For an extra point, who can do the best Tarzan impression?

Round 3: Birds of a Feather

1 Which living bird lays the largest egg?

2 What did the dove return to the Ark with in its beak as a sign that the Flood was over?

3 What is a male chicken called?

4 Which mythical bird is reborn in a fire?

5 What kind of birds were formerly taken down coal mines to test for poisonous gases?

6 Which one of the armed forces formerly had a branch called the Wrens?

7 Which of the following is not a type of sparrow – hedge, house or wall?

Round 4: Pot Luck

1 What is the nickname of the New Zealand rugby league team?

2 What is grown in a paddy field?

3 What is the modern name of the country once called Abyssinia?

4 Who lost all his strength after Delilah cut off his hair?

5 What name do Muslims give to the pilgrimage the faithful are expected to make to Mecca at least once in their lives?

6 Who built Hadrian's Wall?

7 On the banks of which river does Paris stand?

Jackpot

At what age did Alexander the Great die – thirty-three, fifty-three or seventy-three?

✳ Not everyone buried in Poets' Corner was a poet. Also buried there is Thomas Parr, who achieved fame just for being very old. Having married for the second time at the age of 122, he finally died in 1635 supposedly aged 152.

Quiz 42

Round 1: Pot Luck

1 Sumo is a popular sport in which country?

2 Where would one find a jib?

3 Dolphins are more intelligent than humans – true or false?

4 In which sport do teams contest the Calcutta Cup?

5 In *Oliver Twist*, who is the crafty old man who invites Oliver to join his gang of pickpockets?

6 Which regional cooking style produced the fajita?

7 The adjective 'simian' refers to what kind of animals?

Round 2: London Calling

1 In which London park is Speaker's Corner?

2 For what kind of business is London's Savile Row famous?

3 Where is the Unknown Warrior's tomb?

4 What colour plaques identify the London homes of famous people?

5 Who lives at Clarence House?

6 Where in London can one see Traitor's Gate?

7 The Mansion House in London is the official residence of whom?

Half-time teaser

For an extra point, who can make the loudest noise by 'snapping' their fingers?

Round 3: Numbers

1 The opposite faces of dice always add up to which number?

2 In Roman numerals, which letter represents 100?

3 What was the American B-17 bomber better known as?

4 What is half of one-quarter?

5 A snowflake has four, six or eight sides?

6 How many years are there in a millennium?

7 How many are there in a baker's dozen?

Round 4: Pot Luck

1 What is the unit of currency in India?

2 Which marshland bird is famous for its booming call?

3 What colour are gorse flowers?

4 In astronomy, what are classed as spiral, elliptical or irregular?

5 Which country do the Maori come from?

6 The book and film *The Red Badge of Courage* was set during which war?

7 What was the name of the vacuum cleaner in *The Teletubbies*?

Jackpot

What is the average lifespan of a housefly – one day, one week or one month?

✴ Though widely familiar today, the fajita (spiced meat rolled in a tortilla) is a relatively new idea. The first record of the word 'fajita' appearing in print dates back only as far as 1971.

Quiz 43

Round 1: Pot Luck

1 Who became Britain's first female prime minister?

2 Who has nephews called Huey, Dewey and Louie?

3 Of which European country is Belgrade the capital?

4 Whose best friend is Huckleberry Finn?

5 In which fictional town is *Coronation Street* set?

6 Which English city had the Roman name Aquae Sulis?

7 The base of a four-sided pyramid is triangular in shape – true or false?

Round 2: Ships and Shipwrecks

1 The *Titanic* sank after colliding with what?

2 Who journeyed to Antarctica on board the *Discovery* in 1901?

3 Which of the following is not a kind of ship – a barque, a ketch, a chopper or a brig?

4 What name is given to a flat-bottomed Chinese sailing vessel?

5 In Greek mythology, who was the woman whose beauty launched a thousand ships?

6 In which ship did the Pilgrim Fathers sail to the New World?

7 Nelson's flagship *Victory* is now preserved in which port – Southampton, Portsmouth or Falmouth?

Half-time teaser

For an extra point, who can think of the most animals whose name begins with the letter A?

Round 3: Love and Marriage

1 What is the date of St Valentine's Day?

2 Marie Antoinette was married to Napoleon Bonaparte – true or false?

3 Who deserted his wife Jennifer Aniston for Angelina Jolie in 2005?

4 With which Egyptian ruler did the Roman general Mark Antony famously fall in love?

5 In classical mythology, who was Cupid's mother?

6 Which British queen was married to the ill-fated Henry Darnley?

7 Which pop celebrity in 2004 had a marriage that lasted just fifty-five hours?

Round 4: Pot Luck

1 Who was the month of July named after?

2 What colour does litmus paper go when dipped in acid?

3 What should you do with a toupee – wear it, drive it or keep it as a pet? ✻

4 In which location is Judas said to have betrayed Jesus Christ?

5 If a soldier is AWOL, what is he?

6 Who was the central character in *The Once and Future King*?

7 What physical disability did the poets Homer and John Milton have in common?

Jackpot

How many hearts does an octopus have – one, two or three?

✻ Famous owners of toupees over the years have included John Wayne, Humphrey Bogart, Bing Crosby, Frank Sinatra, Jimmy Stewart – and Julius Caesar.

Quiz 44

Round 1: Pot Luck

1 In which city does the Eiffel Tower stand?

2 What kind of animals live in a formicary?

3 Which US president resigned in 1974?

4 What name is given to the art of clipping hedges into decorative shapes?

5 Where is the headquarters of the United Nations?

6 In which war was the Gallipoli campaign fought?

7 In which book does a ship called the *Pequod* feature prominently?

Round 2: Gold and Silver

1 What is the chemical symbol for gold?

2 What was the name of Long John Silver's parrot?

3 Who annoyed Hitler by winning four gold medals in the 1936 Olympics?

4 Where in Britain is the promenade called The Golden Mile?

5 What is a bar of gold known as – a spigot, a maggot or an ingot?

6 Which mythological king suffered the misfortune of seeing everything he touched turned to gold?

7 Which English king met the king of France at the Field of the Cloth of Gold in 1520?

Half-time teaser

For an extra point, who can do the best impression of Arnold Schwarzenegger saying 'I'll be back'?

Round 3: Deep Waters

1 Which is the deepest of the world's oceans?

2 Upon which river does the University Boat Race take place?

3 By what name do the French refer to the English Channel?

4 Which river is spanned by the Clifton Suspension Bridge? ✶

5 In which war did the naval battle of Jutland take place?

6 Which mythological character fell in love with his own reflection in a pool?

7 Which organs enable a fish to breathe underwater?

Round 4: Pot Luck

1 Which 2000 film follows the attempt of a group of chickens to escape from Farmer Tweedy and his wife?

2 What colour do mourners wear at funerals in Eastern countries?

3 Which football team play at the Stamford Bridge stadium?

4 What is the name of the world's second-highest mountain?

5 What did the ancient Egyptians use as paper?

6 Which country was called East Pakistan until 1972?

7 Which trilogy of novels follows the adventures of a young girl called Lyra?

Jackpot

How long does the average dream last – three seconds, thirty seconds or three minutes?

✶ The bridge has a notorious reputation for the number of people who have committed suicide by throwing themselves off it. The story is still told of one young woman who hurled herself from the parapet in 1885, only to float gracefully to the ground on her billowing skirts.

Quiz 45

Round 1: Pot Luck

1 Who, in Greek mythology, was the king of the gods?

2 What kind of creature is Eeyore in *Winnie-the-Pooh*?

3 Which country has the nickname Blighty?✕

4 Which car company has a name that translates from Latin as 'let it be done'?

5 Which of these was not a World War II fighter plane – Hurricane, Lancaster or Typhoon?

6 What can you measure with a protractor?

7 Which leader's rebellion finally ended at Culloden in 1745?

Round 2: Horseplay

1 Who supposedly rode naked on horseback through the streets of Coventry in protest against local taxes?

2 Who had a horse called Bucephalus?

3 Where on a horse would one find a frog?

4 Which famous horse race includes jumps called Becher's Brook and The Chair?

5 In *The Lord of the Rings*, what is the name of Gandalf's horse?

6 What kind of animal is a devil's coach-horse?

7 How does someone on Shanks's pony travel?

Half-time teaser

For the youngest member of each team: For an extra point, who can stick their tongue out the furthest?

Round 3: Crooked Carryings-on

1 Who, in the Sherlock Holmes stories, was called 'the Napoleon of crime'?

2 What means of escape did bank robbers in Paris use for the first time on 27 October 1901?

3 What is the name of the fashion-obsessed villainess in *101 Dalmatians*?

4 By whom was John F. Kennedy's assassin Lee Harvey Oswald shot dead?

5 In which James Bond adventure is Oddjob an evil henchman?

6 What did Dorothy need to steal from the Wicked Witch of the West?

7 In Cluedo, what is the name of the person who has been found dead at the start of the game?

Round 4: Pot Luck

1 Whose motto was 'all for one and one for all'?

2 What is the name of the hometown of the Flintstones?

3 Which team won the first Premier League football championship in 1993?

4 Which great body of water is named after the Greek god Atlas?

5 What is the main ingredient of house dust?

6 What is a male deer called?

7 What does an aeroplane's altimeter measure?

Jackpot

How many countries are there in the world – around 132, around 192 or around 232?

✷ The word came originally from the Hindustani word *vilayati*, which means 'foreign'.

Quiz 46

Round 1: Pot Luck

1 What is a bicycle for two riders called?

2 What is traditionally said to be the equivalent in dog years of one human year?

3 What was the name of the single recorded jointly by Mick Jagger and David Bowie for Live Aid in 1985?

4 Which Mediterranean island is divided into Turkish and Greek sectors?

5 In which part of France did the D-Day landings take place – Burgundy, Normandy or Picardy?

6 Which sport is played by the Harlem Globetrotters?

7 Who was the royal author of the children's story *The Old Man of Lochnagar*?

Round 2: Weird Words

1 What two words were combined to form the word 'motel'?

2 If feline refers to cats, what does ovine refer to?

3 Which popular spread takes its name from the French for 'cooking pot'?

4 Who wears a hat called a mitre?

5 Where was a cat-o'-nine tails used?

6 In which sport might one encounter a googly?

7 What does 'pusillanimous' mean – angry, fearful or untrustworthy?

Half-time teaser

For an extra point, who can do the best impression of a steam train?

Round 3: Music to the Ears

1 When Madonna joined her first pop group, did she start as a singer, a guitarist or a drummer?

2 What kind of musical instrument is a bodhran?

3 In which city was outrageous Black Sabbath lead singer Ozzy Osbourne born?

4 Who wrote the controversial ballet *The Rite of Spring*?

5 Which Welsh singer later switched to pop after enjoying early success with her debut album *Voice of an Angel*?

6 Which boy band has a line-up consisting of Brian, Nick, Howie, A.J. and, until 2006, Kevin?

7 Who shot to fame in 2000 with the debut album *Whoa, Nelly!*?

Round 4: Pot Luck

1 Which park is home to Yogi Bear?

2 Which king of England famously burned some cakes?

3 Who did Pierce Brosnan follow as James Bond?

4 Which state is ruled by members of the Grimaldi family?

5 Who wrote about Jemima Puddleduck?

6 By what name is the condition known as hydrophobia usually known?

7 Which city in India became infamous for its Black Hole?

Jackpot

In which year was the National Lottery launched in the UK – 1990, 1992 or 1994?

✳ Scientists question the validity of this equation. Some have suggested that it would be more accurate to equate the first two years of a dog's life with ten and a half human years each, and each dog year after that with four human years, although this does not take into account a dog's size or breed.

uiz 47

Round 1: Pot Luck

1 Which Italian food has a name that means 'little strings'?

2 What do chandlers make?

3 What is a dik-dik – a motorbike, a watch or an antelope?

4 What was the name of the ship upon which Charles Darwin voyaged to the Pacific?

5 What nationality was the painter Picasso?

6 What colour is the cross on the flag of St George?

7 Which British soap opera is set in Albert Square?

Round 2: Animal Magic

1 In the well-known rhyme, how many magpies for a boy?

2 What apparently miraculous feat can the Jesus Christ lizard perform?

3 Which lizard is best known for changing its colour to match its surroundings?

4 How fast can a cat run – 21, 31 or 41 miles per hour?

5 Which snake expands its neck to warn off threats?

6 Frogs drink and breathe through their skin – true or false?

7 In which George Orwell book is a farm taken over by the animals who live there?

Half-time teaser

For an extra point, who can list the most Harry Potter book titles?

Round 3: Days that Changed History

1 What was introduced to Britain by Sir Walter Raleigh on 27 July 1586?

2 What landmark figure did the world's population pass around 6.33 p.m. on Monday 9 August 1999?

3 Where was the US Pacific Navy attacked by Japan on Sunday 7 December 1941?

4 Which war was triggered by the assassination of Archduke Franz Ferdinand in Sarajevo on 28 June 1914?

5 On 4 February 1504 James IV of Scotland took part in the first officially documented match in which sport?

6 In Easter week of which year was Dublin the scene of a doomed Rising – 1816, 1916 or 1956?

7 In which year was the date nine-eleven significant?

Round 4: Pot Luck

1 What did St George kill the dragon with?

2 How many strings does a violin have?

3 Which travels faster – light or sound?

4 What name was given to the wars fought between the rival houses of York and Lancaster?

5 Who was the creator of Tracy Beaker?

6 Which German commander suffered a reversal in fortunes at El Alamein in 1942?

7 What appears once in a minute, twice in a week and once in a year?

Jackpot

When did the *Titanic* sink after hitting an iceberg – 1902, 1912 or 1922?

✱ Magpies have long been considered bringers of ill luck. One theory is that this relates to an old tradition that the bird refused to wear full mourning black at Christ's Crucifixion. Another claims that a magpie was ejected from Noah's Ark for chattering too much.

Quiz 48

Round 1: Pot Luck

1 Arachnophobia is the fear of what?

2 It is impossible to keep your eyes open when you sneeze – true or false?

3 What nationality is singer Charlotte Church?

4 What do Britains Ltd make?

5 In Hawaii, what is the hula – a dance, a drink or a grass skirt?

6 What is the main constituent of glass?

7 Which instrument did bandleader Glenn Miller play?

Round 2: Movie Matters

1 In the films *Ice Age* and *Ice Age: The Meltdown*, what kind of animal is Manny?

2 Where was Kevin supposed to be with his family in *Home Alone 2*?

3 Which movie monster first climbed the Empire State Building in 1933?

4 In which Italian city does most of the 1969 film *The Italian Job* take place?

5 In which 2005 film was the galaxy engulfed in the Clone Wars?

6 What was the Pink Panther in the first film of that name?

7 In *The Wizard of Oz*, what was the name of Dorothy's dog?

Half-time teaser

For an extra point, who can list the most European countries?

Round 3: Alphabetical Order

1 In the James Bond books and films, by what letter is the officer who provides James Bond with his lethal gadgets known?

2 In Roman numerals, which number is represented by the letter M?

3 Which is the only US state that begins with L?

4 Which letter is positioned between F and H on a computer keyboard?

5 Which letter of the alphabet has a tittle?

6 Can you name the two African countries that have names beginning with Z?

7 No number between one and ninety-nine contains the letter A – true or false?

Round 4: Pot Luck

1 What is the emblem of St Patrick?

2 Who came to the British throne in 1837?

3 What do the initials GPS stand for?

4 Which part of the body is affected by tinnitus?

5 A dog called Montmorency was one of the main characters in which classic book?

6 Which pop group comprising Beyoncé Knowles, Kelly Rowland and Michelle Williams broke up in 2005?

7 Where is the bulk of the USA's gold reserve kept?

Jackpot

How many bones are there in a human backbone – sixteen, twenty-six or thirty-six?

✳Much of the film was shot far from Italy's sunny climes. The end of the famous car chase, in which the three Minis escaped through the sewers, was actually filmed in the sewers of Stoke Aldermoor, a suburb of Coventry.

Quiz 49

Round 1: Pot Luck

1 What is the name of the lion in the Narnia books of C. S. Lewis?

2 Of what was John Logie Baird a pioneer?

3 Which important institution moved to Llantrisant in Wales in 1968?

4 Who is the Hindu goddess of death?

5 Rocky Marciano became famous in which sport?

6 What is the name of the Jedi knight who trains Luke Skywalker in the *Star Wars* films?

7 It is impossible to kill yourself by holding your breath – true or false?

Round 2: Clubs, Groups and Gangs

1 What was founded by Robert Baden-Powell in 1907?

2 Of which secretive organisation was J. Edgar Hoover head?

3 What is a group of witches called?

4 Which US football club did David Beckham leave Real Madrid for in 2007?

5 A group of crows is known as what – a murder, a killing or a conspiracy?

6 By what name is the Religious Society of Friends better known?

7 Which political party was led by Vladimir Ilyich Lenin?

Half-time teaser

For an extra point, who can think of the most famous people from the past whose surname begins with P?

Round 3: Bygone Tymes

1 Which city did the ancient Greeks capture using a wooden horse?

2 In ancient Egyptian mythology, Ra was the god of what?

3 What did the Romans use a hypocaust for?

4 What did a cooper make?

5 What is the name of the Gaulish Druid in the adventures of Asterix?

6 The Domesday Book was compiled during the reign of which king of England?

7 Where did dead warriors go in Norse mythology?

Round 4: Pot Luck

1 What name is given to a beaver's home?

2 What is a thespian interested in?

3 Which two colours are shared by the flags of Argentina, Finland and Greece?

4 In which sport do players contest the Ryder Cup?

5 Which country, in 1976, became the only one to fail to win a gold medal while hosting an Olympic Games?

6 Which king hid in an oak tree after the Battle of Worcester? ✳

7 Which novel by Arthur Conan Doyle featured living dinosaurs?

Jackpot

How many funnels did the *Titanic* have – three, four or five?

✳ The original oak, at Boscobel House, died after tourists removed many of its branches as souvenirs. Its replacement was badly damaged by a storm in 2000, so a new sapling, grown from an acorn from the old tree, was planted by Prince Charles in 2001.

Quiz 50

Round 1: Pot Luck

1 What, in Scotland, is a loch?

2 Oxygen is the largest constituent of the air we breathe – true or false?

3 Who is the odd one out – Churchill, Wilson, Jones, Thatcher, Blair?

4 What was the name of the one-eyed giant of Greek mythology?

5 Who was the first first-class cricketer to score a maximum thirty-six runs in an over?

6 What is a Derringer – a fire extinguisher, a lively dance or a small gun?

7 Which British monarch was on the throne at the time of the Armada?

Round 2: Celebrities

1 The Spice Girls comprised Baby, Ginger, Posh, Scary – and who else?

2 What is the name of Ozzy Osbourne's celebrity wife?

3 Which artist claimed that in the future everybody would be famous for fifteen minutes?

4 In 1994 Michael Jackson became the son-in-law of which deceased pop star?

5 By what name did Katie Price become famous?

6 Who caused a stir in 2006 by adopting David Banda?

7 What surname do Brooklyn, Romeo and Cruz share?

Half-time teaser

For an extra point, who can raise one eyebrow the highest without raising the other?

Round 3: Horror

1 In the story by Robert Louis Stevenson, into whom was Dr Jekyll transformed?

2 Which infamous murderer worked as a barber in Fleet Street?

3 Which innovation alarmed shoppers when introduced for the first time at Harrods in Knightsbridge?

4 Where is Sir Arthur Conan Doyle's *The Hound of the Baskervilles* chiefly set?

5 Which demonic Russian cleric was known as The Mad Monk?

6 What is the name of the fearsome beast that Winnie-the-Pooh attempts to trap in *The House at Pooh Corner*?

7 In which aquatic horror film does one character tell another 'We're going to need a bigger boat'?

Round 4: Pot Luck

1 What shouldn't you eat when there is an R in the month?

2 Which British scientist appears on a £10 note?

3 Where might one find a Plimsoll Line?

4 Modern winners in the Olympic Games receive gold medals, but what did they receive in classical times?

5 Who succeeded Barbara Cartland as the world's best-selling author?

6 Which saint's day falls on 23 April?

7 Which television character has the catchphrase 'yeah but no but yeah but'?

Jackpot

What percentage of the human brain is water – 10 per cent, 50 per cent or 80 per cent?

✴ The person who first said it eventually became so tired of being asked about it, he tried to confuse interviewers by rephrasing it variously as 'In the future fifteen people will be famous' and 'In fifteen minutes everybody will be famous'.

Quiz 51

Round 1: Pot Luck

1 When are nocturnal creatures active?

2 Which Greek scientist is famous for shouting 'Eureka!'?

3 In motor racing, what name is given to a series of tight bends?

4 Which famous outlaw was shot by Pat Garrett in 1881?

5 Which of the following artists was not Dutch – Rembrandt, Gauguin or Van Gogh?

6 Honshu is one of the islands making up which country?

7 In the 1957 book by Dr Seuss, what did the Grinch steal?

Round 2: Odd One Out

1 Which is not a kind of frog – marsh frog, edible frog or leapfrog?

2 Which is the odd one out – Cardiff, Edinburgh or Manchester?

3 Which does not have four sides – a square, a rectangle or a triangle?

4 Which is the odd one out – basil, mint, marjoram, nettle or sage?

5 Which is the odd one out – Madrid, Lisbon, Barcelona or Seville?

6 Which of the following was not a poet – John Keats, John Mills or John Milton?

7 Which of the following is not a martial art – kendo, judo or Cluedo?

Half-time teaser

For the youngest member of each team: For an extra point, who can be first to point to something yellow?

Round 3: Heavy Metal

1 What was the Duke of Wellington's nickname – the Steel Baron, the Brass Earl or Iron Duke?

2 Which came first – the Iron Age or the Bronze Age?

3 What is a mixture of two metals called?

4 Which metal is also a nickname for a policeman?

5 Which medieval science was concerned with the transformation of base metals into gold?

6 Pewter consists of between 85 per cent and 99 per cent of which metal?

7 Which is more valuable – gold, silver or platinum?

Round 4: Pot Luck

1 What is the name of the hero in J. R. R. Tolkien's *The Hobbit*?

2 What does the U stand for in UN?

3 What was Bonnie Prince Charlie's surname?

4 Which desert extends over a large area of northern China and south-eastern Mongolia?

5 From whose reign does Jacobean architecture date?

6 Which is the only continent that does not have an active volcano?

7 Which grow faster – fingernails or toenails?

Jackpot

What is the current world record for running 100 metres backwards – 13.6 seconds, 16.6 seconds or 23.6 seconds?

✷ For many years it was believed that the outlaw in question was left-handed, based on the evidence of a photograph in which he wears his gun holster on his left hip. It was only relatively recently that it was realised that the photograph had been created by means of a process in which the image is reversed, meaning he was in fact right-handed.

Quiz 52

Round 1: Pot Luck

1 What is a dried plum called?

2 What is the aerial sport played by two teams of seven players in the Harry Potter novels of J. K. Rowling?

3 Which US state is bordered by Arizona, Nevada and Oregon?

4 What sex are drone honeybees?

5 What comes in bladderwrack and kelp varieties?

6 Which two oceans are linked by the Panama Canal?

7 In 2007 Nicolas Sarkozy became president of which country?

Round 2: Husbands and Wives

1 Who is the wife of the puppet character Punch?

2 How many of Henry VIII's wives were beheaded?

3 Which comedian is married to Dawn French?

4 In which country was Elizabeth II's husband Prince Philip born?

5 Which actress married tennis player John McEnroe in 1986?

6 Which US film actor married Welsh actress Catherine Zeta-Jones in 2000?

7 What is the name of Homer Simpson's wife?

Half-time teaser

For an extra point, who, in one minute, can think of the most words containing the word 'hand'?

Round 3: Bad Ends

1 Which series of children's books follows three children sent to live with relatives after their parents are killed in a fire?

2 How did the Italian dictator Mussolini die – by shooting, by hanging or of old age?

3 What happened to the witch who made Hansel and Gretel prisoners in her gingerbread house?

4 The Roman emperors Tiberius and Claudius, Tsar Alexander I of Russia and Charles V of France all died after eating what?

5 In which forest was the English king William Rufus shot by an arrow while hunting?

6 Which ruler of ancient Egypt died after being bitten by an asp?

7 In *James and the Giant Peach*, what had happened to James's parents?

Round 4: Pot Luck

1 The poet William Wordsworth is most often remembered for lines written about which flowers?

2 How many m's are there in 'minimum'?

3 What is a caribou – an antelope, a reindeer or a moose?

4 Which country is home to the Nobel Prize committee?

5 In which year of the twentieth century were there three British kings?

6 In which Shakespeare play is Shylock a central character?

7 What should one do with a brioche – put it on one's foot, eat it or put it back in the river?

Jackpot

What is the maximum speed reached by a raindrop – 8, 18 or 80 miles per hour?

✶Incidentally, as four of Henry's marriages were annulled, meaning they never took place legitimately, it could be argued that technically he only ever had two wives.

Quiz 53

....

Round 1: Pot Luck

1 Not all birds can fly – true or false?

2 In which country is Abu Simbel an important archaeological site?

3 Terry Pratchett's *Discworld* novels began with *The Colour of* – what?

4 Which is the UK's highest military decoration?

5 What are Oxford bags?

6 With which sport is Wimbledon internationally associated?

7 What is three times fifty?

....

Round 2: Freshwater Facts

1 Which US river has the nickname 'Old Man River'?

2 Which of the following rivers empties into the Mediterranean – the Rhine, the Danube or the Nile?

3 In which water sport might one 'catch a crab'?

4 Which of the following is a river in Africa – the Volga, the Volvo or the Volta?

5 Who teamed up with Paul Simon on the album *Bridge Over Troubled Water*?

6 The river Lagan reaches the sea at which Northern Ireland city?

7 What is the correct spelling of the Great Lake called Lake Erie?

....

Half-time teaser

For an extra point, who can make up the funniest name by combining the name of a vegetable with that of a piece of clothing?

....

Round 3: Warlocks, Witches and Wizards

1 What colour is traditional for a witch's cat?

2 In *The Wizard of Oz*, how did the Wicked Witch of the East die?

3 What is the real name of Jill Murphy's *Worst Witch*?

4 Who was the star of Disney's 'The Sorcerer's Apprentice' from *Fantasia*?

5 Which time of day is known as 'the witching hour'?

6 Which waterlogged spirit is supposed to have enchanted the wizard Merlin, casting him into an everlasting sleep?

7 What domestic implement do witches supposedly use to fly on? *

Round 4: Pot Luck

1 What colour is a sunflower?

2 Which military rank is more senior – brigadier or colonel?

3 Who was the creator of Jeremy Fisher?

4 Which murderer terrorised the East End of London in 1888?

5 What is a kumquat – a weapon, a fruit or a tent used by nomads?

6 Which is Britain's smallest bird?

7 Where do most accidents take place – in the car, in the street or in the home?

Jackpot

How many people are recorded to have died in the Great Fire of London – none, six or 1666?

* The thought of witches flying around their homes used to frighten many people. One recommended means of protection from such activity was the ringing of church bells – it was widely believed that witches could not stand the sound of bells and would crash to the ground.

Quiz 54

Round 1: Pot Luck

1 Which ingredient makes bread rise?

2 Who became known as the Widow of Windsor?

3 Which sport has the largest playing area – polo, water polo or hurling?

4 The Khyber Pass links Afghanistan with which other country?

5 To which country does the Rock of Gibraltar belong?

6 What, in medieval times, was a sackbut – a large barrel, a musical instrument or a person with a big bottom?

7 What is the left side of a ship called?

Round 2: Names

1 Which country was known to the Romans as Helvetia?

2 On which item might one see the name Steinway?

3 What is the name of the galaxy to which Earth belongs?

4 Which is not a name for a male chicken – rooster, pullet or cockerel?

5 What was the real name of the Maid of Orleans?

6 Which US sportsman with the first names Orenthal James hit the headlines off the sports field in 1994?

7 What was the name of the German air force during World War II?

Half-time teaser

For an extra point, who can repeat the tongue-twister 'Red lorry, yellow lorry' five times quickly without making a mistake?

Round 3: Gardens

1 In which garden did Adam and Eve meet?

2 What is the American name for a garden?

3 What was the nickname of garden designer Lancelot Brown?

4 Which county is known as the Garden of England?

5 What is the popular garden shrub buddleia commonly known as – the caterpillar bush, the bug bush or the butterfly bush?

6 Whose statue was placed in Kensington Gardens in 1912?✳

7 Which best-selling garden-related book was the work of Frances Hodgson Burnett?

Round 4: Pot Luck

1 What is the name of the person who directs an orchestra – the controller, the connector or the conductor?

2 How many are there in a dozen?

3 What is the name of the temple on the Acropolis in Athens?

4 To which city were Geoffrey Chaucer's pilgrims going?

5 Do tears taste salty, sugary or vinegary?

6 What is the official language of Mozambique?

7 By what name is the Boeing 747 better known?

Jackpot

In which year is the last wild wolf in Britain said to have been killed – 1543, 1643 or 1743?

✳Kensington Gardens, previously the private gardens attached to Kensington Palace, became very popular after being opened to the public. When the king asked what it would cost to have them made private again, his prime minister replied 'A crown.'

Quiz 55

Round 1: Pot Luck

1 Which part of the body does an optician treat?

2 What is the American term for a pavement?

3 Which is the odd one out – cappuccino, Assam or espresso?

4 Who composed the *Enigma Variations*?

5 In which European country is Catalan spoken?

6 For what was Mata Hari famous – as a writer, a Hawaiian queen or a spy?

7 What do giant pandas live on?

Round 2: The Abbreviated Version

1 What do the initials SOS stand for?

2 In computing, what is a CPU?

3 What abbreviation is used for Self-Contained Underwater Breathing Apparatus?

4 What does the DC stand for in Washington, DC?

5 In military jargon, what was a DUKW? ✳

6 In text messaging, what does MYOB mean?

7 What does PTO stand for?

Half-time teaser

For an extra point, who, without looking at one, can draw the best picture of the 'tails' side of a standard 50p coin? (Clue if needed: it has a woman and a lion on it.)

Round 3: Catchphrases

1 Whose catchphrase is 'Can we fix it? Yes, we can'?

2 Which popular TV comedy introduced the catchphrase 'Lovely jubbly'?

3 Which British politician said he would be 'tough on crime and tough on the causes of crime'?

4 With which quiz show might one associate the phrases 'fifty-fifty' and 'ask the audience'?

5 Who has the catchphrase 'Nice to see you, to see you nice'?

6 Which newspaper has the motto 'All human life is there'?

7 Which spacecraft had a five-year mission 'to boldly go where no man has gone before'?

Round 4: Pot Luck

1 What is the study of living organisms called?

2 The Seychelles are situated in which ocean?

3 What nationality was the poet Dylan Thomas?

4 Who was the last president of the Soviet Union?

5 Who provided the voice of Shrek?

6 Where was the Battle of Britain primarily fought – in the air, at sea or underground?

7 Of which country was Robert the Bruce king?

Jackpot

In which year was a horse race first decided by a photo finish (nearest answer wins)?

✶ The name had no connection with the animal. The D denoted the year it was first made (1942), while the U stood for 'utility', the K meant 'four-wheel drive' and the W indicated that it had two powered rear axles.

Quiz 56

Round 1: Pot Luck

1 What does a carnivorous animal eat?

2 Who were Athos, Porthos and Aramis?

3 What might one do with a blunderbuss – drive it, fly it or fire it?

4 Which modern country once formed the larger part of Roman Gaul?

5 Which musical features the song 'You'll never walk alone'?

6 Who is the comedian behind Ali G and Borat?

7 The Chicago Bulls are a leading side in which sport?

Round 2: Hands and Feet

1 In which hand does the Statue of Liberty hold her flaming torch?

2 Which north European country is associated with the wearing of clogs?

3 How many bones are there in the human hand – seven, seventeen or twenty-seven?

4 Which animal is commonly measured in hands?

5 Which of the following do not have webbed feet – frogs, herons or seagulls?

6 Which tendon in the foot is named after an ancient Greek hero?

7 Which footballer became notorious for scoring a goal that he credited to 'the hand of God'?

Half-time teaser

For an extra point, who, with their eyes closed, can bring their outstretched hands together so that their the tips of their little fingers meet?

Round 3: Arch-enemies

1 Whose arch-enemies include Lex Luthor?

2 Who opposed the Union forces in the US Civil War?

3 Which crop has an enemy called the Colorado beetle?

4 What was the name of the cat who was always trying to catch Tweety Pie?

5 Which Chicago gangster became, in 1930, America's first 'public enemy number one'?

6 Which animal is noted for its ability to kill deadly snakes – the wombat, the meerkat or the mongoose?

7 Whose arch-enemies included Mordred and Morgan le Fay?

Round 4: Pot Luck

1 Which falling fruit is said to have inspired Newton's theory of gravity?

2 Who was the Norse god of mischief?

3 Who was murdered in Canterbury Cathedral in 1170?

4 Which is longer – the Panama Canal or the Suez Canal?

5 Who wrote the adventure novels *Ivanhoe* and *Rob Roy*?

6 What is the national sport of Canada?

7 The okapi is the only known relative of which well-known African animal?∗

Jackpot

In which year were the first Matchbox cars sold – 1943, 1953 or 1963?

∗The rare okapi only became known to the rest of the world in 1902, after Sir Harry Johnston, the British governor of Uganda, rescued some pygmies from being captured by a German showman, who intended to exhibit them in Europe. The grateful pygmies helped Sir Harry obtain the skull and skin of an okapi, thus enabling its identification.

Quiz 57

Round 1: Pot Luck

1 What is Ben Nevis – a mountain, a Scottish footballer or a large bell?

2 What is the correct spelling of 'tomorrow'?

3 Can you complete the novel title *Pride and* – ?

4 To which family of animals does the hyrax belong – mammals, birds or reptiles?

5 In which country do Ajax play domestic football?

6 What instrument does Vanessa Mae play?

7 How many pockets does a snooker table have?

Round 2: Alphabet Soup

1 What do Americans call the letter zed?

2 Which three capital letters have no straight lines?

3 What do the letters RAC stand for?

4 What does the W in the initials SWAT, as in SWAT team, stand for?

5 In electronics, what do the initials LCD stand for?

6 British tanks are usually given names beginning with which capital letter?

7 Which is the only sign of the zodiac that begins with the letter G?

Half-time teaser

For an extra point, what is 190 plus 70 minus 4?

Round 3: Fire and Water

1 What is the emperor Nero said to have done while Rome burned in 64 AD?

2 Which is the longest river in the world?

3 Who was the Roman god of fire?

4 Where might one find an oasis – in an ocean, in a desert or up a mountain?

5 Which is the largest of the Great Lakes?

6 What burst into flame in the 1974 film *The Towering Inferno*?

7 In which ocean is the Sargasso Sea?

Round 4: Pot Luck

1 Where was the prophet Muhammad born?

2 In which US state is Boston?

3 Which country won soccer's World Cup in 2002?

4 What kind of animal lives in a drey?

5 What modern name is now given to the ancient country of Persia?

6 What name did the Romans give to the Greek goddess Aphrodite?

7 If you are mad, what kind of animals do you have in your belfry?

Jackpot

In which year was the first traffic roundabout constructed in the UK – 1909, 1939 or 1959? ✶

✶ As originally installed, traffic could opt to go round Letchworth's Sollershott Circus roundabout either clockwise or anticlockwise, depending upon whether the driver wished to turn left or right, but this was later changed.

Quiz 58

Round 1: Pot Luck

1 How many weeks are there in a year – forty-eight, fifty-two or sixty?

2 What replaced the British Empire in 1931?

3 Which pharaoh's tomb was located by British archaeologist Howard Carter in 1922?

4 What is the main ingredient of marzipan?

5 Is a skunk a variety of weasel, raccoon or badger?

6 Which US athlete was stripped of Olympic gold in the 100 metres in 1988?

7 Which animal is mentioned more frequently than any other in the Bible?

Round 2: Flags and Anthems

1 What colour is the cross on the Scottish flag of St Andrew?

2 What is the name of the French national anthem?

3 What colour appears with white in the national flag of Japan?

4 Which of the following is not one of the colours on the Irish flag – green, blue or orange?

5 Of which country is 'The Star-spangled banner' the national anthem?

6 What do the five rings on the Olympic flag represent?

7 What name is given to the military ceremony during which a regiment's flags are paraded?

Half-time teaser

For an extra point, in two minutes, who can list the most two-letter words?

Round 3: Cats and Dogs

1 How many lives are cats said to have?

2 What was the dog in Enid Blyton's Famous Five called?

3 In the poem, who set sail with the pussycat in a pea-green boat?

4 Which breed of large dog was bred for mountain rescue work in Switzerland?✳

5 In Greek mythology, what was the name of the three-headed dog that guarded the entrance to Hades?

6 What is the name of the talking cat in the TV series *Sabrina the Teenage Witch*?

7 According to the proverb, what killed the cat?

Round 4: Pot Luck

1 Botany Bay is located on which continent?

2 What comes in Cos, Romaine and iceberg varieties?

3 Which organisation is known as the TA for short?

4 Where might one find a yardarm – in a playground, on a saucepan or on a mast?

5 In which sport is a team led by a skip?

6 Picasso's masterpiece *Guernica* depicted the effects of bombing in which war?

7 Neither chimps nor baboons have tails – true or false?

Jackpot

In which year was the first space shuttle flight made – 1975, 1981 or 1985?

✳Few people realise that modern dogs of this breed are quite different from the original version and are rarely of any use as mountain rescue dogs today. This is because of a disastrous avalanche many years ago in which most of the dogs used for breeding purposes were killed. The breed has consequently been mixed with other breeds since then.

Quiz 59

Round 1: Pot Luck

1 Which of the following could fly – a velociraptor, a pterosaur or a triceratops?

2 The snatch and the jerk are disciplines in which sport?

3 Who wrote an autobiography called *Just Williams*?

4 In which country does the River Rhine have its source – France, Germany or Switzerland?

5 Which neighbouring country did Iraq invade in 1990?

6 Which army rank is the most senior – captain, lieutenant or major?

7 Which country was formerly ruled by tsars?

Round 2: Foreign Lingo

1 Which language gave English the words 'dinghy', 'juggernaut' and 'shampoo'?

2 Which French phrase refers to something that has been, or is felt to have been, seen before?

3 What do Australians call a billabong – a small furry animal, a kind of boomerang or a pool?

4 What do Mongolians call a yurt – a type of yoghurt, a yobbish youth or a temporary shelter?

5 What is a polonaise – a creamy sauce, a slow dance or a small mint with a hole in it?

6 Which town, formerly called Joppa and now a suburb of Tel Aviv, gave its name to a type of orange?

7 What is a fedora – a type of house, a small dog or a hat?

Half-time teaser

For an extra point, who can give the best impression of a Dalek?

Round 3: Tops and Bottoms

1 On a computer keyboard, which is the only vowel not found on the top row?

2 What is the main ingredient of the topping in Welsh rarebit?

3 What are a black bottom, a cakewalk and a hay?

4 Which Hollywood heart-throb starred in the 1986 film *Top Gun*?

5 Which Shakespeare play features a weaver called Bottom?

6 Who wrote the 1934 hit song 'You're the top'?

7 Which bottom becomes one of Harry Potter's best friends?

Round 4: Pot Luck

1 What is a sequoia?

2 Which country has the highest murder rate in the world?

3 How old was Boris Becker when he became the youngest-ever Men's Singles Champion at Wimbledon in 1985?

4 Which animal is known as 'the ship of the desert'?

5 Which kind of meat can come in entrecôte, fillet or sirloin varieties?

6 What was the name of the ship in which Sir Francis Drake sailed against the Armada?∗

7 Of which African country is Nairobi the capital city?

Jackpot

How many books are there in the Old Testament – thirty-nine, forty-nine or fifty-nine?

∗Visitors to Drake's old home, Buckland Abbey, can still see his famous drum, which is said to beat to an unseen hand whenever England is in danger. Among other occasions, it was apparently heard to sound at the outbreak of World War I in 1914 and again during the Dunkirk evacuation in World War II.

Quiz 60

Round 1: Pot Luck

1 A giraffe cannot cough – true or false?

2 In which museum can you see the *Mona Lisa*?

3 Who succeeded Sir John Betjeman as Poet Laureate in 1984?

4 What kind of animal is an ibex?

5 Where are the Apennine mountains?

6 From which sport comes the saying 'three strikes and you're out'?

7 What emblem do England rugby union players wear on their shirts?

Round 2: The Seven Seas

1 Cuba is an island in which sea?

2 Which sea borders on Egypt, Sudan, Eritrea, Ethiopia, Djibouti, Saudi Arabia and Yemen?

3 Which sea would you have to cross to get from south-east Asia to the Philippines?

4 Which two seas are linked by the Suez Canal?

5 The Irish Sea lies to the west of Ireland – true or false?

6 La Manche is the French name for which body of water?

7 Where is the Sea of Tranquillity?

Half-time teaser

For an extra point, who can make up the best first line for a scary story?

Round 3: Big Bangs

1 What was the name of the volcano off Java that exploded in 1883, making the loudest noise in recorded history?

2 Who wrote the children's novel *Chitty Chitty Bang Bang*?

3 Which is the most crowded country in the world?

4 What was a Brown Bess – a large bomb, a big cannon or a musket?

5 Where does bhangra music come from – West Africa, the West Indies or India/Pakistan?

6 Guy Fawkes was part of which conspiracy to kill the king of England?

7 Whose catchphrase is 'Boom, boom!'?

Round 4: Pot Luck

1 What kind of animal is a flying fox?

2 By what name is the hop, skip and jump known as an official sport?

3 How was Charles I killed – was he hanged, shot or beheaded?

4 Who, in 1946, finally conceded that he was not a god?

5 What is a charleston – a hat, a flower or a dance?

6 Who was the first emperor of Rome?

7 A chipolata is a type of what – chip, sausage or biscuit?

Jackpot

When were dog licences dropped in the UK – 1968, 1978 or 1988?

✳ The theft of the painting in 1911 caused consternation: among those questioned on suspicion of having stolen it was the artist Pablo Picasso. The real thief turned out to be an Italian employee of the museum, who kept the painting in his home for two years before trying to sell it to the Uffizi gallery in Florence and finally being unmasked.

Quiz 61

Round 1: Pot Luck

1 What are forget-me-nots?

2 Kathmandu is the capital of which country?

3 What are Scouts between the ages of six and eight called?

4 Which country was known to the Romans as Lusitania?

5 Which ballet features a Sugar Plum Fairy?

6 After whom did the Three Blind Mice run?

7 How many s's are there in 'success'?

Round 2: Location, Location, Location

1 Glasgow stands on the banks of which river?

2 Who wrote a series of children's stories set in Toyland?

3 In which river was Jesus baptised?

4 Where is Tipperary – Ireland, South Africa or Australia?

5 In which modern country might one find the ruins of ancient Carthage?

6 Which country is located nearest to the North Pole?

7 Which New York street is the centre of commercial theatre in the USA?

Half-time teaser

For an extra point, who can draw the most perfect circle without lifting their pen or pencil off a piece of paper? ✶

Round 3: Eyes and Ears

1 What is a private eye?

2 Which 1933 invention is said to have saved more lives on the road than anything else?

3 What kind of animal comes in eared, elephant and grey varieties?

4 Frogs have no ears – true or false?

5 Does a grasshopper have two, five or twelve eyes?

6 According to the Bible, it is easier to get what kind of animal through the eye of a needle than it is for a rich man to enter heaven?

7 What shape are Mickey Mouse's ears?

Round 4: Pot Luck

1 Which is the highest mountain in Wales?

2 Which of the following is a breed of dog – red kite, red setter or red Angus?

3 Which colour comes in Van Dyke, burnt sienna and umber varieties?

4 How were Elizabeth I and Mary, Queen of Scots related?

5 Which business tycoon presents British television's *The Apprentice*?

6 Which plant offers relief from nettle stings?

7 Which sport has an 'extra cover' and a 'silly mid-on'?

Jackpot

In which year were the first Oscars awarded – 1929, 1939 or 1949?

✷ When Pope Benedict was trying to decide, in the fourteenth century, which artist to give an important commission to, he asked for samples of their work as proof of their talent. The great artist Giotto, instead of providing a detailed drawing or painting, drew a simple, perfect circle. The pope, realising how difficult it is to draw a perfect circle, readily acknowledged the artist's skill.

Quiz 62

Round 1: Pot Luck

1 What is a female deer called?

2 Which fish of the Amazon basin is notorious for devouring deer, humans and other creatures?

3 Who was the last of the reigning Stuart kings and queens of Britain?

4 What name did Rhodesia take when it won independence from Britain in 1980?

5 Which Japanese city was the first to be destroyed with an atomic bomb?

6 Which Asian country was formerly under the rule of the Dalai Lama?

7 How many days are there in four weeks?

Round 2: Planetary Bodies

1 Which comet returns to Earth every seventy-five years?

2 On how many other planets in the universe have scientists detected life?

3 Which planet in our solar system has moons all named after characters from Shakespeare – Jupiter, Uranus or Saturn?

4 Jupiter consists solely of gas – true or false?

5 Which astronomical body officially lost planetary status in 2006 due to its small mass?

6 Which is the hottest planet in the solar system?

7 Which superhero worked as a reporter on *The Daily Planet*?

Half-time teaser

For an extra point, who can spell 'Mississippi'?

Round 3: Bear Truths

1 After whom were teddy bears named?

2 Pandas are not bears – true or false?

3 Where might one find the Little Bear, the Charioteer and the Crab?

4 What is the name of the injured bear used to promote BBC Children in Need events? ✶

5 By what English name is the Ursa Major constellation also known?

6 Which golfer is nicknamed the Golden Bear?

7 All polar bears are left-handed – true or false?

Round 4: Pot Luck

1 What is carried in arteries and veins?

2 Which one of King Arthur's knights found the Holy Grail?

3 'The Red-Headed League' and 'The Speckled Band' are stories about which fictional detective?

4 What does a cartographer do?

5 What is the British name for what the Americans call a 'zucchini'?

6 Which modern sport developed from a game called battledore?

7 Which is lowest – a soprano, alto or tenor voice?

Jackpot

On which Mediterranean island was the Minoan civilisation based – Crete, Cyprus or Malta?

✶The bear was actually named after a town in Yorkshire, where the grandfather of Joanna Ball, creator of the mascot, once served as mayor.

Quiz 63

Round 1: Pot Luck

1 How many humps does a Bactrian camel have?

2 The Grand Canyon is located in which US state?

3 What comes in rag, hearth and Turkish varieties?

4 In American slang, what is a 'gumshoe'?

5 What is a pyrophobic person frightened of?

6 Which children's toy was inspired by Hawaiian dancing?

7 A worm has two heads – true or false?

Round 2: Desert Islands

1 Which fictional character spent twenty-eight years on a desert island after being shipwrecked in 1659?

2 Which of the following is an island off Africa – Liberia, Madagascar or Sierra Leone?

3 On which Caribbean island is the US base of Guantanamo?

4 On which remote island in the South Atlantic did Napoleon die in 1821?

5 What was the name of the deranged castaway in Robert Louis Stevenson's *Treasure Island*?

6 What is the name of the Caribbean island divided between the Republic of Haiti and the Dominican Republic?

7 On which Pacific island did the artist Paul Gauguin paint his most famous works?

Half-time teaser

For an extra point, who, in two minutes, can name the most British cities and towns beginning with the letter B?

Round 3: Old Wives' Tales

1 Which number is considered the unluckiest?

2 According to the rhyme, what is Friday's child?

3 How many years of bad luck does a person supposedly get if they break a mirror? *

4 Can you complete the rhyme: 'See a pin and pick it up, all the day you'll have – ' what?'

5 Which colour, according to superstition, is the unluckiest for cars?

6 In which country is the leprechaun a mischief-making supernatural being?

7 At which end should a boiled egg be opened – the bigger end or the smaller end?

Round 4: Pot Luck

1 What is a coracle – a boat, a form of coral or a long story?

2 On which river does New York City stand?

3 Who, in 2006, ended his career holding the record for goals scored in the Premiership?

4 In Greek mythology, who was the winged messenger of the gods?

5 Which Scandinavian city was formerly called Christiania?

6 The Gurkhas come from which country – India, Tibet or Nepal?

7 What kind of an animal is a mynah – a snake, a fish or a bird?

Jackpot

What percentage of all known animals have backbones – 3 per cent, 33 per cent or 66 per cent?

* Most people know this superstition, but few people remember what the antidote is. Apparently, if you hold the broken bits of mirror under running water the bad luck is all washed away.

Quiz 64

Round 1: Pot Luck

1 According to the proverb, what comes before a fall?

2 Who might use a hod – a soldier, a bricklayer or a vet?

3 What is the name of the ritual dance performed by New Zealand's international rugby team before the start of play?

4 Which king of England was the son of Mary, Queen of Scots?

5 Which Egyptian god of the dead was depicted with the head of a jackal?

6 In which sport do teams contest the Ashes?

7 What name is given to the five-sided headquarters of the US Department of Defense?

Round 2: Points of the Compass

1 In which direction does the Sun rise?

2 Which is furthest east – Denmark, Norway or Sweden?

3 Which country in Africa boasts the continent's most northerly point?

4 What name is given to the imaginary line that divides the northern and southern hemispheres?

5 Which country lies to the immediate south of Egypt?

6 Lizard Point marks which furthermost point of the UK – the western, the eastern or the southern?

7 Which is furthest south – Dover, Southampton or Penzance?

Half-time teaser

For the youngest member of each team: For an extra point, who can do the best impression of a monkey?

Round 3: Ringing the Changes

1 In the *Stars Wars* saga, into whom is Anakin Skywalker transformed?

2 By what name was the Indian city of Mumbai formerly known?

3 What name is given to the pupal stage of a butterfly?

4 Which country was formerly known as Formosa?

5 What was the name of the controversial Windscale power station changed to?

6 Who succeeded Margaret Thatcher as prime minister in 1990?

7 Who, in 2006, decided he had had enough of being married to Heather Mills?

Round 4: Pot Luck

1 In which of the following countries is the euro not the official national currency – France, the UK or Italy?

2 Which US city includes boroughs called Brooklyn and the Bronx?

3 Who of the following has never been prime minister – Gordon Brown, Neil Kinnock or Tony Blair?

4 Where might one find an apse – in a theatre, a church or an aircraft?

5 What do Americans call the autumn?

6 Of which country was Zog I the last king?

7 The Arctic surrounds the South Pole – true or false?

Jackpot

How many years did it take Michelangelo to paint the ceiling of the Sistine Chapel – four, fourteen or forty?

✶The dance comes in more than one version. The older version, which lacks the controversial throat-slitting gesture of the version introduced in 2005, was inspired by the cunning of a Maori chieftain who hid from his enemies in a food-pit concealed by an old woman's wide skirt.

Quiz 65

Round 1: Pot Luck

1 In which sport is it possible to achieve a hole-in-one?

2 What kind of seabird comes in Arctic, common, little and Sandwich varieties?

3 Who was the leader of Italy's redshirts?

4 In rugby union, the Wallabies represent which nation?

5 Which gladiator led a slave rebellion against the Roman Empire in 73 BC?

6 In cockney rhyming slang, what are 'apples and pears'?

7 By what name is sodium chloride better known?

Round 2: Movie Madness

1 What are Hollywood's Academy Awards informally known as?

2 From which film did the song 'Chim chim cheree' come?

3 Which film was advertised with the slogan 'An adventure 65 million years in the making'?

4 What rank was held by the Ryan that Tom Hanks sought to save in 1998?

5 Which 2007 Disney film was about a rat who wants to be a chef?

6 Which film star appeared in the role of Rocky Balboa for the sixth time in 2006?

7 Who wrote the book on which the musical *Oliver!* was based?

Half-time teaser

For an extra point, who (without writing it down) can spell abracadabra backwards without making a mistake? ✳

Round 3: Treemendous Trees

1 Which dark-leaved evergreen tree is traditionally planted in churchyards?

2 What kind of trees do dates and coconuts grow on?

3 Dylan Thomas's most famous poetic work concerned characters living under what group of trees?

4 Which South American mammal spends most of its time hanging motionless upside down from tree branches?

5 Which kind of tree produces conkers?

6 Which kind of tree did Charles II hide in?

7 Aintree is home to which famous horse race?

Round 4: Pot Luck

1 Who defeated Edward II at Bannockburn?

2 Apart from Bolivia, which is the only country in South America with no coastline?

3 A dugong is a bird with a large curved bill – true or false?

4 Which Mediterranean island is the historical home of the Mafia?

5 Scientist Albert Einstein was once offered the post of president of which country?

6 Which nursery rhyme character had a great fall off a wall?

7 Which grows to the largest size – a tuna, a sardine or a pilchard?

Jackpot

How many seconds make up one hour – 6300, 3600 or 630?

✳ The word abracadabra has been considered magical for centuries. People often carried charms with the word written on to ward off fever, toothache and even the plague. It is thought to have been derived from the Hebrew words for Father (*Ab*), Son (*Ben*) and Holy Spirit (*Ruach Acadosch*).

Quiz 66

Round 1: Pot Luck

1 On which continent are the Atlas Mountains?

2 What is a TKO in boxing?

3 Desiree and King Edward are varieties of what?

4 What is Tracey Emin famous as?

5 What is the British equivalent of an American condominium?

6 During which war did the battles of Brandywine, Lexington and Saratoga take place?

7 What is another name for a parenthesis?

Round 2: Black and White

1 Dalmatian dogs are born all black – true or false?

2 What does it mean if officials wave a black flag at a Formula One driver's car?

3 Which small black-and-white mammal defends itself by emitting an unbearable smell?

4 Which band's best-selling records include one known as *The White Album*?

5 Who is lead singer with the rock band Black Sabbath?

6 Which golfer is nicknamed the Great White Shark?

7 Which white mountain is the highest peak in the Alps?

Half-time teaser

For an extra point, what is 75 times 2, minus 20 plus 3?

Round 3: Songs and Singers

1 Which singer said no, no, no to rehab in 2007?

2 According to the 1988 song by Bobby McFerrin, don't worry, be – what?

3 Who were the champions of the world in 1977?

4 Who, in 1998, asked for permission to entertain you?

5 How long do the wheels on the bus go round and round?

6 Who, in 2000, let the dogs out?

7 Where, in the music hall song, did I invite you to come and make eyes at me?

Round 4: Pot Luck

1 Which is more senior – an earl or a baron?

2 Which is nearest to Dover – Calais, Cherbourg or Le Havre?

3 Where on the body might one find a whorl?

4 Which wartime leader appeared on posters with the slogan 'Your Country Needs You'?

5 Which English aristocrat was 'mad, bad and dangerous to know'?

6 Which international humanitarian organisation was founded in Geneva in 1863?

7 Which country has a famous Foreign Legion?

Jackpot

Where was badminton first played – Scotland, Canada or India?

＊Bad though it is, modern scientists have created even worse stinks. These include the notorious 'Who-Me', a foul-smelling liquid created during World War II with the idea that members of the French Resistance could smear it on their German invaders, thus humiliating them.

Quiz 67

Round 1: Pot Luck

1 Is a minuet a very brief moment of time, a small car or a dance?

2 Which is an orchestral instrument – the French horn, the German horn or the Belgian horn?

3 In which country did the Solidarity trade union eventually take power?

4 What is a capercaillie?

5 From which British city do the Kaiser Chiefs hail?

6 Which cricket ground has a Nursery End and a Pavilion End?

7 Which is the only continent upon which strawberries are not grown?

Round 2: Water, Water Everywhere

1 Which inland sea is bordered by Russia, Turkey and Romania among other countries?

2 How many high tides are there in twenty-four hours?

3 In which country are the Angel Falls, the highest free-falling waterfall in the world – Australia, Venezuela or Zambia?

4 Which of the following does not live in the sea – a red admiral, a blue marlin or a grey nurse?

5 Which of the following grows on rocks and boat hulls – manacles, binnacles or barnacles?

6 Which Sir Francis sailed single-handed round the world in *Gypsy Moth IV*?

7 The main part of an iceberg is usually under water – true or false?

Half-time teaser

For an extra point, who, with their eyes closed, can draw the best man or woman?

Round 3: Hats Off

1 What are boaters traditionally made from?

2 What name is given to the square, flat hat worn by university scholars?

3 Who is always depicted wearing a floppy red hat trimmed with white fur?

4 What kind of headgear is a lobster pot?

5 What shape did a 1920s cloche hat have?

6 What is the wide-brimmed hat of Mexican peasants called?

7 Where might one find a high hat – on a policeman, on a Viking or in a drum kit?

Round 4: Pot Luck

1 Of which African country beginning with R is Kigali the capital?

2 Which meat is used to make chilli con carne?

3 In which war did the International Brigade play an important role?

4 What is a taipan – a Japanese tiepin, a Thai cooking pot or a snake?

5 For which team did Wayne Rooney play before joining Manchester United?

6 Which fruit was originally known as the love-apple?

7 According to the poem, what will you be if you can keep your head when all around you are losing theirs?

Jackpot

How many children did Queen Victoria have – five, seven or nine?

＊The band borrowed their name from a South African football club also called the Kaiser Chiefs. The link was the captain of the local English football team, who once played for the South African side.

Quiz 68

Round 1: Pot Luck

1 Which one of the Mr Men is a practical joker who lives in a teashop-shaped house and drives a shoe-shaped car?

2 Which great work of English literature includes 'The Knight's Tale'?

3 In cricket, what name is given to a lower-order batsman sent in to protect a key player late in the day?

4 Which city served as the first capital of the USA?

5 Who was the British monarch during World War I?

6 How many square centimetres are there in one square metre?

7 Egyptian is the chief language spoken in Egypt – true or false?

Round 2: All Shapes and Sizes

1 How many faces does a cube have?

2 How many sides are there to a parallelogram – three, four or five?

3 Which is biggest – a megabyte, a kilobyte or a gigabyte?

4 With which sizeable crime was Ronnie Biggs linked?

5 The Great Orme and the Little Orme are geographical features in which part of the UK?

6 How many sides does a 50p piece have (without looking)?

7 What are scissors with sawtoothed, zigzagged edges called?

Half-time teaser

For an extra point, who, in just one minute, can think up the most rhymes for 'man'?

Round 3: Vile Villains

1 Who is Peter Pan's Eton-educated sworn enemy? ✳

2 Ernst Stavro Blofeld is one of which hero's most evil enemies?

3 Which writer created the villains Bill Sikes, Magwitch and Uriah Heep?

4 Which fairy-tale hero is threatened by the evil Abanazar?

5 Whose enemies include the evil Green Goblin and Doctor Octopus?

6 What is the name of the tiger who seeks to kill Mowgli in *The Jungle Book*?

7 Which fictional character is hunted by the villainous Sheriff of Nottingham?

Round 4: Pot Luck

1 What is the name of the RAF aerobatic display team?

2 Who said, when entering US customs, 'I have nothing to declare but my genius'?

3 The Inquisition was part of which major church?

4 Which artist's favourite subjects included cornfields and sunflowers?

5 By what other name is the kookaburra known?

6 Which of the following is not situated on the coast – Marseille, Paris or Bordeaux?

7 Which of the following is not a fish – haddock, halibut or habbakuk?

Jackpot

How many baths did Louis XIV of France take during his lifetime – none, four or forty-four?

✳ *Peter Pan* author J. M. Barrie once gave a lecture at Eton about its notorious former pupil. Among other nuggets, he revealed that the arch-villain had been very fond of the works of the Lake District poets, loved music and liked flowers. His last words were 'Floreat Etona', the school motto.

Quiz 69

Round 1: Pot Luck

1 Who was the last Anglo-Saxon king of England?
2 In which Indian city did Mother Teresa become noted for her work among the poor?
3 What is half of 116?
4 Who, in World War II, was the Forces' Sweetheart?
5 Which country was formerly known as Cathay?
6 Against whom did Senator McCarthy conduct a campaign in the 1950s?
7 What do zoologists study?

Round 2: Food

1 What food is traditionally eaten on Burns Night?
2 Which cartoon character gets his superhuman strength from spinach?
3 What kind of Japanese food comprises vinegared rice, often topped with raw seafood?
4 What two words were combined to form the word 'brunch'?
5 If you bit into an Elegant Lady, what would you be eating?
6 What kind of food is pumpernickel?
7 If a Cornishman offered you some yarg, what would you be eating?

Half-time teaser

For an extra point, in two minutes, who can list the most plant and flower names beginning with D?

Round 3: Fun and Games

1 Which piece must be taken or trapped to win a game of chess?

2 Card games were invented by the Romans – true or false?

3 How many squares are there on one side of a Rubik's cube?

4 How many spots are there on a pair of dice?

5 How many hoops are needed in a game of croquet?

6 In snooker, which colour ball is potted last?

7 Wild Bill Hickock, Al Jolson and Buster Keaton all died while engaged in what leisure activity?

Round 4: Pot Luck

1 JFK airport serves which US city?

2 Which character delivered the catchphrase 'Don't panic!' in the television comedy series *Dad's Army*?

3 What charge must motorists pay to drive into central London?

4 Which composer wrote the *Ring* cycle?

5 Which one of these is not an event in the decathlon – the long jump, the javelin or the 800 metres hurdles?

6 Which English novelist worked as a child in a boot-blacking factory?

7 What do Americans call a waistcoat?

Jackpot

For how many years did the US Civil War last – four, fourteen or forty?

✷ The story goes that the idea that spinach promotes physical strength dates back to an early report that credited the food with ten times its actual iron content. The misprint leading to this mistake was discovered in the 1930s but was not widely reported until 1981.

Quiz 70

Round 1: Pot Luck

1 Which book begins 'The Mole had been working very hard all the morning, spring-cleaning his little home'?

2 What is the main ingredient of satay sauce?

3 In which sport is the King George V Cup contested?

4 Which US state has just one syllable in its name?

5 In which modern country are the ruins of Troy?

6 Who wrote the *Gormenghast* trilogy?

7 What did the US president Benjamin Harris, who left office in 1893, have that no US president has had since?

Round 2: Opposites

1 What is the opposite of 'slow'?

2 Which country faces Spain across the Strait of Gibraltar?

3 What is the opposite of 'illiterate'?

4 What part of a ship is the opposite of the bow?

5 Who starred opposite Leonardo Di Caprio in *Titanic*?

6 Which creature stands opposite the unicorn on the royal coat of arms?

7 What is the opposite of 'weak'?

Half-time teaser

For an extra point, who can be first to list three words with a letter Z in them?

Round 3: Chinese Whispers

1 How many animals are there in the Chinese calendar of the years?

2 Which of the following does not share a border with China – Mongolia, Vietnam or South Korea?

3 Which of the following is not a river in China – the Yangtze, the Yukon or the Yellow River?

4 What name is given to the district containing the former imperial palace in Beijing?

5 Which British-run territory was returned to China in 1997?

6 Which mythical creature was once a symbol of Chinese emperors?

7 Which sea separates China from North and South Korea?

Round 4: Pot Luck

1 Which nursery rhyme character stuck his thumb into a pie and pulled out a plum?

2 In which country is the battlefield of Waterloo located?

3 What is the infield area called in baseball?

4 Which chemical element has the symbol K?

5 By what name did Joseph Merrick become known – the Lizard Man, the Elephant Man or the Rabbit Man?

6 Which is the only English place name to appear in the title of a Shakespeare play?

7 How many holes are there on a full professional golf course?

Jackpot

In which year did Britain's Great Train Robbery take place – 1953, 1963 or 1973?

✳ The whereabouts of the historical Troy have been generally accepted since the 1870s, but Troy is still otherwise shrouded in legend. According to some, Brutus, the legendary first English king, was a descendant of the Trojan hero Aeneas. The Brutus Stone, a stone set in the pavement in Fore Street, Totnes, Devon, marks the place where Brutus first arrived in England.

Quiz 71

Round 1: Pot Luck

1 What term describes the leading female singer in an opera?

2 Who painted *The Laughing Cavalier*?

3 How many i's are there in 'mischievous'?

4 Where might one find a flying buttress – on a ship, in an aircraft or on a building?

5 Can you complete the play title *A Streetcar Named* – ?

6 Where does the Fastnet Race take place – on the land, on the sea or in the air?

7 The Rio Grande forms the border between the USA and which other country?

Round 2: Musical Instruments

1 Which of the following instruments has strings – a harpsichord, a glockenspiel or a concertina?

2 On which musical instrument would one find frets – a flute, a guitar or a French horn?

3 Which wind instrument is associated chiefly with Australian Aboriginals?

4 What kind of instrument includes among its component parts a bag, a chanter and a drone?

5 Which kind of instrument is associated with the Gibson and Fender brands?

6 How many strings does a Jew's harp have?

7 What kind of instrument is an ocarina – a wind instrument, a string instrument or a keyboard instrument?

Half-time teaser

For an extra point, who can list three of the four counties of England that begin with the letter D?

Round 3: Pets' Corner

1 Dogs are colour-blind – true or false?

2 Which pet can come in angora, pygmy and cottontail varieties?

3 From which continent do alpacas and llamas come?

4 Which Roman emperor considered making his horse Incitatus a consul of Rome? ✳

5 Which herb is particularly loved by cats?

6 Which sign of the zodiac is represented by a goat?

7 Cavies are also commonly known by what other name?

Round 4: Pot Luck

1 What is the American term for petrol?

2 Which artist born in Salford became famous for his 'matchstick' figures?

3 Which singer is often described as the Queen of Soul?

4 The Magna Carta was signed by which English king?

5 How do you spell 'rhythm'?

6 From which sport does the phrase 'no holds barred' come?

7 What, according to a 2004 survey, is a Briton's favourite smell?

Jackpot

In which year did the first man land on the Moon – 1962, 1969 or 1972?

✳ It is said that the horse was provided with a grand house with a full complement of servants, to which important dignitaries were invited to dine with their host, who himself wore a jewel-studded collar and ate from an ivory manger.

Quiz 72

Round 1: Pot Luck

1 In which sport might one encounter a birdie or a fairway?

2 Who wrote a poem beginning 'Tyger! Tyger! burning bright'?

3 Which children's charity was launched by Esther Rantzen in 1986?

4 Where are British army officers trained?

5 Which European country has the most inhabitants – France, Germany or the UK?

6 Who formed the rock band Wings after leaving the Beatles?

7 What is 1001 minus 12?

Round 2: Nations of the World

1 What is the capital of Japan?

2 Which country has the largest army in the world?

3 Audrey Hepburn, Pieter Brueghel and Jean-Claude Van Damme all came from which country?

4 The country of Andorra lies between France and which other country?

5 Who called the English 'a nation of shopkeepers'?

6 On which continent might be found the country of Suriname?

7 Which of the following countries is a kingdom – Egypt, Tunisia or Morocco?

Half-time teaser

For an extra point, who can name the most of the thirteen countries of South America?

Round 3: Colours of the Rainbow

1 What is the traditional colour of British fire engines?

2 On which continent is there an Orange River?

3 Which colour links fever, river and canary?

4 Which colour is called *vert* in French?

5 What colour uniforms did troops loyal to the Union generally wear in the US Civil War?

6 What was the original source of indigo dye – plants, powdered rock or crushed beetles?

7 Violet Beauregarde, Veruca Salt and Augustus Gloop are characters in which children's book?

Round 4: Pot Luck

1 What are guppies, anchovies and minnows?

2 Which European city has a famous St Peter's Square?

3 Which Scottish football club plays at the Ibrox Stadium?✻

4 On which British island is Carisbrooke Castle?

5 Who solved crimes in company with the Hardy Boys?

6 Who was the first woman to rule England as queen in her own right – Anne, Elizabeth or Mary?

7 What does a vintner sell?

Jackpot

How old was Elizabeth II when she was crowned – seventeen, twenty-seven or thirty-seven?

✻ Ibrox is the name of the local district in which the stadium was built. The name comes from Gaelic, in which it means 'badger's sett'.

Quiz 73

Round 1: Pot Luck

1 Which of the following is a popular ball sport – squish, squash or squat?

2 Is a dhow a cooking implement, an agricultural tool or a kind of boat?

3 Which popular musical was based on George Bernard Shaw's play *Pygmalion*?

4 Which treaty formally ended World War I?

5 Which instrument did Louis Armstrong play?

6 Which country lies to the south of Afghanistan?

7 What is a kitchen on a ship known as?

Round 2: Boffinology

1 What is H_2O?

2 If you divide 100 by five and add five – what are you left with?

3 What does a vulcanologist study?

4 A 'bergy bit' and a 'growler' are size classifications of what?

5 Who is remembered for his theory of relativity?

6 What was developed in the Manhattan Project?

7 What does the A stand for in DNA?

Half-time teaser

For an extra point, who can say 'The sixth sick sheikh's sixth sheep's sick' the quickest, without making a mistake?

Round 3: Arms and Legs

1 What is the popular name for a fruit machine operated by the pulling of an arm or lever? *

2 Which English king was commonly depicted with a crooked back and withered arm?

3 Which is the only animal to have four knees?

4 Which part of the UK has a symbol comprising three legs joined together?

5 Which musical instrument features in the royal arms?

6 How many arms does an octopus have?

7 Which have more legs – centipedes or millipedes?

Round 4: Pot Luck

1 Which is the largest of the ape family?

2 What was the name of the Doctor Who assistant played by Billie Piper?

3 In which sport was Babe Ruth a legendary figure?

4 Which country has the longest coastline?

5 Which kind of bird comes in bald, fish and golden varieties?

6 What is the British name for what Americans call a 'diaper'?

7 Which fruit is cider made from?

Jackpot

In which year did Britain recognise American independence – 1776, 1783 or 1812?

* If you have ever wondered why fruit machines have pictures of cherries and melons on them, this is because an early variety of fruit machine offered prizes of chewing-gum, the various flavours of which were illustrated on the rotating drums. The BAR symbol began life as a logo of the Bell Fruit-Gum Company.

Quiz 74

Round 1: Pot Luck

1 How many carats are there in pure gold?

2 Which British airport acquired a controversial fifth terminal in 2008?

3 What is the Royal Worcester factory famous for making?

4 What kind of acid is found in the stomach – hydrochloric acid, sulphuric acid or formic acid?

5 Which of the following battles was not fought on English soil – Blenheim, Sedgemoor or Naseby?

6 Which Spanish football club won the European Championship every year from 1956 to 1960?

7 What is a mandrake – a plant, a gardening rake or a male duck?

Round 2: Birds

1 Which of these is a real bird – the secretary bird, the chairperson bird or the tealady bird?

2 According to the proverb, a bird in the hand is worth two in the what?

3 Which kind of bird comes in mute, trumpeter and whooper varieties?

4 Which legendary film director made the films *The Birds*?

5 Which of the following is not a bird – a shrike, a skate or a skua?

6 What kind of bird does the Ancient Mariner kill in Samuel Taylor Coleridge's poem 'The Rime of the Ancient Mariner'?

7 What are young swans called?

Half-time teaser

For an extra point, who can think up the best name for a new sports car?

Round 3: Snacks

1 According to a recent poll, which flavour of crisps is most often found in the lunchboxes of British children?

2 How were doughnuts allegedly improved in 1847?

3 When is Simnel cake eaten?

4 What is the British name for what Americans sometimes call a 'weenie'?

5 What is a Bath Oliver?✶

6 Which snack has a name that means 'bitter water'?

7 US president Ronald Reagan famously kept a jar of what kind of sweets on his desk in the White House?

Round 4: Pot Luck

1 Which Gilbert and Sullivan opera is set in Japan?

2 What is the name of the ferryman who in Greek mythology rows the dead across the Styx?

3 Which animals leave droppings called spraints?

4 Which country is situated between Switzerland and Spain?

5 Which of the following is in Europe – Mauretania, Mozambique or Moldova?

6 In which sport is the Davis Cup contested?

7 How many u's are there in 'vacuum'?

Jackpot

What percentage of a jellyfish is water – 50 per cent, 75 per cent or 95 per cent?

✶ The creator of this foodstuff was, logically enough, a certain Doctor Oliver of Bath, in Somerset. When Doctor Oliver died he left the recipe to his coachman, who used it to make his fortune, remembering his benefactor in the name of his product.

Quiz 75

Round 1: Pot Luck

1 Which classic children's toy has the full name Barbara Millicent Roberts?

2 Which Anglo-Saxon king made Wessex the dominant power in England in the ninth century?

3 The Dunhill Cup is contested in which sport – cricket, golf or tennis?

4 Vanilla is derived from a variety of which family of plants?

5 Which state most recently became part of the USA?

6 What is the main period of fasting in the Muslim religion called?

7 How many days are there in a leap year?

Round 2: Money Matters

1 How many cents are there in a US dollar?

2 What colour is a ten-euro note – grey, red or blue?

3 What is the national currency of Japan called?

4 What new form of money was introduced in Switzerland in 1661?

5 Which type of animal comes in money, house and trapdoor varieties?

6 In which European country is the zloty the national currency?

7 How many sides are there to a 20p coin?

Half-time teaser

For the youngest member of each team: For an extra point, who can be first to point out something beginning with D?

Round 3: Demons, Devils and Saints

1 Which is a traditional name for the Devil – Mick, Dick or Nick?

2 Is a Tasmanian devil a carnivorous marsupial, a whirlwind or a cocktail?

3 Who was the author of *The Satanic Verses*?

4 Who is the patron saint of lost causes?

5 After which saint is Newcastle United's ground named?

6 Who is the patron saint of Scotland and Russia?

7 Which popular firework is named after a saint?

Round 4: Pot Luck

1 Is a baobab a type of monkey, a tree or a chocolate and banana pudding?

2 In which part of the body might the patella be found?

3 What are the rows of life-size model soldiers found in the tomb of the early Chinese emperor Shi Huangdi called?

4 What kind of fish is a rollmop made with?

5 In which novel is Alan Breck a fugitive from the English?

6 Which of the following does not have a Mediterranean coastline – Turkey, Israel or Iran?

7 In which sport is the Super Bowl played? ✳

Jackpot

Who to date has been the oldest person to ascend the throne of Britain – Queen Victoria, William IV or Lady Jane Grey?

✳ The name Super Bowl was never intended as a permanent name for the event but just to be used temporarily until something better was suggested. Coined in the 1970s, it combined a reference to the Rose Bowl game contested by US colleges and the bouncy Super Ball toys then very popular with children.

Quiz 76

Round 1: Pot Luck

1 What is the botany the study of?
2 Which of the following is not a vegetable – an onion, a tomato or a cabbage?
3 Which country has the largest number of Catholics – Italy, France or Brazil?
4 By what name did the Irishman Fingal O'Flahertie Wills become better known?
5 With which organs does a person absorb oxygen into the bloodstream?
6 Who among the disciples was the brother of Peter?
7 What is the correct spelling of 'separate'?

Round 2: Sporty Numbers

1 How many finger-holes are there in a tenpin bowling ball?
2 How many motorbikes usually compete in a speedway race?
3 Who is the only footballer to have played more games for Manchester United than Bobby Charlton?
4 How many attempts can a high-jumper make at a particular height?
5 How many people are there in an American football team?
6 Which country was admitted to rugby union's Five Nations Championship in 2000, making it the Six Nations Championship?
7 How many points are awarded to the winner of a Formula One race?

Half-time teaser

For an extra point, in two minutes, who can think of the most words beginning with 'un-'?

Round 3: Sur le Continent

1 Madrid is the capital of which European country?

2 In which European city is there a famous Doge's Palace?

3 Which European country do the French call L'Ecosse?

4 In which European country was the first motorway opened – France, Germany or the UK?

5 Which European country was invaded by the Soviet Union in 1968?

6 Which South American country has a name that means 'little Venice'?

7 How was the European Economic Community halved in geographical size in 1981?

Round 4: Pot Luck

1 Which is the only play by Shakespeare set in Scotland?

2 Which children's book has characters called Homily, Pod and Arrietty?

3 Which band had a hit in 1999 with 'Why does it always rain on me?' – Coldplay, Blur or Travis?

4 Which type of animal includes edible, robber and spider varieties?

5 Which English county has its administrative headquarters at Taunton?

6 What is a quarter of 444?

7 Which of the following was not one of the knights of the Round Table – Kevin, Gawain or Galahad? ✶

Jackpot

In degrees Celsius what is the normal body temperature of a healthy adult – 27°C, 37°C or 47°C?

✶ It should be noted that the actual number of knights varies from one source to another, from twelve to as many as 150 or more. The famous Round Table preserved in Winchester details twenty-five knights, but this table dates only from the late thirteenth century, long after the mythical King Arthur's time.

Quiz 77

Round 1: Pot Luck

1 Whose band of friends included Friar Tuck and Little John?

2 Which sporting activity features giant slalom and downhill races?

3 How many countries does France share a border with – three, eight or ten?

4 In *Alice in Wonderland*, what are used as mallets in a game of croquet?

5 How many of Henry VIII's wives survived him?

6 What instrument measures atmospheric pressure?

7 What is a trawler – a type of aircraft, a boat or a lorry?

Round 2: It's in the Blood

1 Which blood type is the most common – A negative, O or AB?

2 The Bloody Tower and the White Tower are parts of which London building?

3 What is William Harvey remembered for discovering?

4 How many litres of blood are there in the average human body?

5 Which Irish rock band had a hit with the song 'Sunday Bloody Sunday'?

6 Which carry blood away from the heart – arteries, veins or glands?

7 What is the name of Mickey Mouse's pet bloodhound?

Half-time teaser

For an extra point, how many letters are there in 'supercalifragilisticexpialidocious'?

Round 3: Wardrobe Wonders

1 Where might one wear a Stetson – on one's foot, on one's head or round one's waist?

2 Who wears a tutu – a ballet dancer, a builder or a vicar?

3 Which German immigrant, in 1853, made the world's first pair of jeans? *

4 Which biblical character had a coat of many colours?

5 Which actress caused a stir in 1994 wearing a black Versace dress fastened with gold safety pins?

6 Who wrote the fairy tale 'The Emperor's New Clothes'?

7 What is the American name for a dinner jacket?

Round 4: Pot Luck

1 Which precious stones are judged by colour, clarity, cut and carat?

2 Of which country is Brussels the capital?

3 What was the name of the last Russian tsar?

4 Which footballer remains unique in scoring a hat-trick in a World Cup final?

5 In cockney rhyming slang, what is referred to as 'bees and honey'?

6 Which kind of sea creature is known for its bark?

7 What was the name of the capital city in the Land of Oz?

Jackpot

In which country is the Atacama desert – Chile, China or Chad?

* The person in question had arrived in San Francisco at the height of the California gold rush. Prospectors spotted the rough canvas he was selling for use as tents and wagon covers and suggested that it would be better employed to make trousers, as the only ones otherwise available quickly wore out. The first jeans were thus intended for gold prospecting.

Quiz 78

Round 1: Pot Luck

1 What is the southernmost tip of South America called?

2 Which two countries are connected by the Channel Tunnel?

3 In which sport does the playing area include a 'popping crease'?

4 The Chinook, the Diablo and the Fremantle Doctor are all what?

5 What is a pinafore – a type of dress, a small boat or a kind of pineapple?

6 Who do Americans sometimes call the 'Father of his Country'?

7 What does the word *pokemon* mean?

Round 2: Farmyard Animals

1 What is a male goose called?

2 From which animal does mutton come?

3 Which farmyard animal is considered sacred in India?

4 The disastrous Bay of Pigs invasion of 1961 took place in which country? ✶

5 Which animals like to bray?

6 Which fictional pig had best friends called Fly, Ferdinand and Farmer Hoggett?

7 What is a young goat called?

Half-time teaser

For an extra point, who can draw the best horse?

Round 3: Into the Unknown

1 Where do Wallace and Gromit venture for a picnic in *A Grand Day Out*?

2 Which great explorer had a flagship called *Santa Maria*?

3 Which Venetian trader opened up links with distant China in the thirteenth century?

4 What kind of journeys begin at Cape Canaveral?

5 Which European explorer discovered Hawaii?

6 Who sailed to the Antarctic in 1914 in HMS *Endurance*?

7 Who was the first person to walk on the Moon?

Round 4: Pot Luck

1 What was a Penny Black – a coin, a boiled sweet or a stamp?

2 On which island is the volcano Mount Etna?

3 Nellie Melba was world-famous as what – a singer, a dancer or a cook?

4 Which king of France died on the guillotine during the French Revolution?

5 Which kind of creature is carved into the hillside at Uffington, Oxfordshire?

6 Which country underwent a Cultural Revolution in the 1960s?

7 What is the British equivalent of what Americans call 'sneakers'?

Jackpot

Which country in the world has the most post offices – China, India or the USA?

＊The bay is not, incidentally, noted for its many pigs. The English name of the bay probably resulted from a mistranslation of the Spanish original, which is thought to refer not to the local pigs but to the bay's many triggerfish.

Quiz 79

Round 1: Pot Luck

1 What is the longest coral reef in the world called?

2 What is the name of Dick Dastardly's dog?

3 To which country does Bermuda belong?

4 Turtles have no teeth – true or false?

5 By what name did the writer Samuel Langhorne Clemens become famous?

6 In which Charlotte Brontë novel is the ten-year-old central character sent to the inhuman Lowood school?

7 What is the birthstone for November – garnet, ruby or topaz?

Round 2: Fancy Footwork

1 Where is the flamenco a traditional dance?

2 What kind of animal starred in the 2006 film *Happy Feet*?

3 Which South American country was the birthplace of the tango?

4 Molly, Cotswold and Border are all styles of which English folk dance?

5 In the musical and film *Billy Elliot*, what does Billy's father initially hope Billy will become?

6 Irish step dancing enjoyed a massive revival in the 1990s as a result of which hit dance show?

7 Which long-running British television show pairing celebrities with professional dancers was first screened in 2004?

Half-time teaser

For an extra point, who can do the best American accent?

Round 3: Splash Happy

1 Which modern British artist is famous for paintings of splashes in swimming pools?

2 Who was the first person to swim the English Channel?

3 Which aquatic team sport made its debut as an Olympic event in 1984?

4 In which ocean did Apollo 11 splash down after the first manned mission to the Moon?

5 In which sport might a competitor execute an Eskimo roll?

6 According to the Bible, how long did the Great Flood last – 40 days, 100 days or 150 days?

7 What name is given to a grotesque carving on a church or other building that serves as a gutter for rainwater?

Round 4: Pot Luck

1 What event in 1981 attracted the largest-ever British TV audience?

2 What was the name of Romulus's brother?

3 In 1967, which British football club became the first to win the European Championship?

4 In which Italian city may one see Leonardo da Vinci's *Last Supper*?

5 The Opium War of 1839 involved which two countries?

6 Who wrote the long-running play *The Mousetrap*?

7 The Mount of Olives stands outside which Middle Eastern city?

Jackpot

Which has the loudest call of all land animals – the bittern, the howler monkey or the hyena?

✴ The various birthstones are all supposed to have unique magical properties. Opal is among the most powerful – among other things, it is said to help hair to keep its colour longer if worn by blondes.

Quiz 80

Round 1: Pot Luck

1 Which continent is home to the biggest bird, the fastest land animal and the largest land animal?

2 From which animal does venison come?

3 What colour is ebony wood?

4 What is calligraphy concerned with – handwriting, California or volcanoes?

5 To which group of artists did Degas, Manet, Monet and Renoir belong?

6 In which TV series are Edie, Susan, Lynette, Gabrielle and Bree neighbours?

7 In which novel do children called Peter, Phyllis and Roberta enjoy life on the tracks?

Round 2: Music Mayhem

1 How many musicians are there in a quintet?

2 Which song is said to be sung more frequently than any other?

3 Which city in Tennessee is considered the home of country music?

4 How many times has the UK won the Eurovision Song Contest – never, three times or five times?

5 How many notes are there in an octave – eight, ten or twelve?

6 Which long-running British music programme was cancelled in 2006, forty-two years after it started?

7 What is the name of the bugle call that traditionally ends the day in the British army?

Half-time teaser

For an extra point, who can name the most of Snow White's Seven Dwarfs?

Round 3: Famous Families

1 What is the name of Elizabeth II's youngest son?

2 Which of the following was not one of the famous literary Brontë sisters – Agnes, Emily or Charlotte?

3 What was the name of the self-proclaimed holy man who exercised great influence over the Russian royal family before the 1917 Revolution?✳

4 In which popular television drama series were the Ewings the star family?

5 Of which Italian city were the Medici family rulers for 300 years?

6 Indira and Rajiv were assassinated members of which famous political family?

7 Which television family originally comprised Norma, Jim, Barbara, Denise and Antony?

Round 4: Pot Luck

1 What creatures live in a hive?

2 What is the full title of NATO?

3 Would one wear a sou'wester when it is hot, when it is cold or when it is wet?

4 What nationality was the fairy-tale writer Hans Christian Andersen?

5 In which field of the arts was Henry Moore an acclaimed figure?

6 Which kind of oil is used to treat cricket bats?

7 What is the correct spelling of 'rhubarb'?

Jackpot

Mecca is a city in which country – Iraq, Saudi Arabia or Egypt?

✳The person in question was eventually murdered, but he proved a hard man to kill. He is said to have remained stubbornly alive after being poisoned with cyanide, shot several times and clubbed and only died after being thrown into the icy Neva River. Interestingly, the autopsy reports indicate that he was actually killed by the third shot, allegedly fired by a British officer called Oswald Rayner.

Quiz 81

Round 1: Pot Luck

1 Where might one encounter a bosun – on an aircraft, on a boat or on a person's head?

2 How many Catherines did Henry VIII marry?

3 Who composed the music for the ballet *Swan Lake*?

4 Which city was known to the Romans as Lutetia?

5 The Strait of Messina separates mainland Italy from which island?

6 Which of the following is not part of a plant – carpals, sepals or Urals?

7 Which animal is thought to kill more human beings than any other animal on the African continent?

Round 2: Bricks and Mortar

1 What are Inuit igloos constructed with?

2 What kind of building might be looked after by a sexton?

3 Which building toy was first developed in Denmark in 1949 by Ole Kirk Christiansen?

4 Where might one find a barbican, a curtain wall and loop windows?

5 In which city was St Michael's Cathedral destroyed by bombs in November 1940?

6 Which city includes among its buildings the Gherkin, Tower 42 and the O$_2$ Arena?

7 How many levels does a bungalow have?

Half-time teaser

For an extra point, who can say 'unique New York' the fastest, three times, without making a mistake?

Round 3: Them Bones

1 What does an invertebrate lack?

2 What is the British equivalent of what Americans call 'the crazy bone'?

3 Which part of the body contains a femur?

4 Whereabouts in the human body is the one bone that is not connected to any other?

5 What is the more common name for the scapula?

6 How many bones are there in the adult human body – 106, 206 or 306?

7 Which of the following has no backbone – a lobster, an eel or a lizard?

Round 4: Pot Luck

1 What is 10 per cent of 120?

2 By what name was sharpshooter Martha Jane Burke better known?

3 What is the British name for what Americans call a 'bullhorn'?

4 What colour is the pigment chlorophyll?

5 During which battle were tanks first used on 15 September 1916? ✶

6 What is the full title of BAFTA?

7 Which is a kind of orange – a mandolin, a mandarin or a mandrake?

Jackpot

Which is the odd one out – magenta, cerulean or Peruvian?

✶ The name 'tank' was chosen deliberately in order to disguise the true nature of the British Army's new secret weapon, the idea being to convince spies the vehicles were meant for carrying water. They were also referred to early in their development as 'landships'; other names considered included 'motor-war car' and 'cistern'.

Quiz 82

Round 1: Pot Luck

1 Which sea creatures produce pearls?

2 Who compete for the Turner Prize – musicians, writers or artists?

3 Which rock band features the brothers Liam and Noel Gallagher?

4 Which English county has its administrative headquarters at Matlock?

5 What do Americans call aluminium?

6 What did Germany call its submarines in the two world wars?

7 What is a quarter of twenty?

Round 2: Bright Ideas

1 Which US inventor is usually identified as the inventor of the light bulb?

2 What did type of pen did László Bíró invent – the ballpoint pen, the felt-tip pen or the fountain pen?

3 Which sport was invented by William Webb Ellis in 1823?

4 When was the crossword invented – 1853, 1913 or 1953?

5 For whom did Humphry Davy invent a famous lamp?

6 Which fictional inventor became famous for his 'cracking contraptions'?

7 Which British inventor invented a wind-up radio?

Half-time teaser

For an extra point, who can toss a coin and get heads the most times in ten throws?

Round 3: A Word in Your Ear

1 What word can come before fly, race and box?

2 'Charm' is the collective name for a group of what – fish, goldfinches or kittens?

3 What is the correct spelling of 'accommodate'?

4 What would one do with a hurdy-gurdy – ride it, wear it or play it?

5 What does 'wysiwyg' stand for? ✳

6 What are brogues – shoes, trousers or gloves?

7 Which of the following words is a palindrome – moon, noon or soon?

Round 4: Pot Luck

1 What form of transport is involved in the Tour de France – bicycles, horses or motor cars?

2 Which fictional doctor learned how to talk to animals?

3 Who wrote the music for fourteen of W. S. Gilbert's comic operas?

4 Of which country is Budapest the capital?

5 Which of the following does not narrate one of the *Canterbury Tales* – the friar, the miller or the soldier?

6 Which word for uncontrollable fear comes from the name of an ancient Greek god?

7 Which country does Paddington Bear come from?

Jackpot

Which of the following is not on the south coast – Southampton, Eastbourne or Southend-on-Sea?

✳ 'Wysiwyg' is but one of many examples of modern business jargon. Don't be surprised if you hear an entrepreneur saying he is 'getting his ducks in a row' (putting things in order), 'halving his footprint' (reducing his workforce) or 'pushing the peanut forward' (making progress).

Quiz 83

Round 1: Pot Luck

1 In a pack of playing cards, how many cards are there in a suit?

2 What is pewter – a sort of metal, a strong-smelling flower or furniture for churches?

3 What is the name of Russell Crowe's sailing ship in *Master and Commander*?

4 What do the letters 'AKA' stand for?

5 In 2007, which British racing driver finished second in the Formula One championship in his debut season?

6 With which English hero was Emma Hamilton associated?

7 Which of the following is not a style of dance – the polka, the salsa or the jodhpur?

Round 2: Great Players

1 In football, who holds the record for England caps?

2 In which sport did Olga Korbut excel – swimming, gymnastics or weightlifting?

3 With which sport might one associate Fischer, Korchnoi, Karpov and Short?

4 Which record did Roger Bannister break in 1954?

5 In which country was England cricketer Kevin Pietersen born?

6 Whose drop goal sealed England's victory in the 2003 Rugby World Cup?

7 What number did Brazilian soccer star Pelé wear on his shirt when playing for his country?

Half-time teaser

For an extra point, who can put the following in correct historical order – the Wars of the Roses, the Norman Conquest, the Cold War, the English Civil War, World War I?

Round 3: Famous Addresses

1 Where did King Arthur hold court over the Round Table?

2 What was the name of Elvis Presley's home in Memphis?

3 Who lived at 221b Baker Street? ✳

4 Who lives at 11 Downing Street?

5 Which football team's home is Old Trafford?

6 Who works at Lambeth Palace?

7 What is No. 1 Canada Square better known as?

Round 4: Pot Luck

1 What is formed by the impact of a meteorite?

2 Which city has the nickname 'Auld Reekie'?

3 How many girls are there in the Spice Girls?

4 Which county lies between Norfolk and Essex?

5 Which of the following is not a cheese – edam, demerara or mozzarella?

6 Which is not a type of pasta – lasagne, macaroni or timpani?

7 What is the name of the holy book of Islam?

Jackpot

Who was the last ruler of Britain who could not speak English – George I, George II or William IV?

✳ Various modern buildings have laid claim to being 221b Baker Street, though in reality at the time the address first became famous the real Baker Street ended at number 100.

Quiz 84

Round 1: Pot Luck

1 What is an Islamic place of worship called?

2 How many times have Italy won football's World Cup?

3 Who was head of the Nationalists in the Spanish Civil War?

4 Which slab of rock, now in the British Museum, proved the key to understanding Egyptian hieroglyphics?

5 Which country is ruled from the Kremlin?

6 Can you complete the title of the novel by E. M. Forster *A Passage to* – ?

7 What physical feature distinguishes terrapins, tortoises and turtles?

Round 2: Film Facts

1 Where was the trilogy *The Lord of the Rings* filmed?

2 Who played the US president in the 1997 film *Airforce One*?

3 In the film *Polar Express*, what does the boy ask for when offered a gift by Santa Claus?

4 In which film series did Michael J. Fox star as Marty McFly?

5 Which country took offence when made fun of by comedian Sacha Baron Cohen in the 2006 film *Borat*?

6 Which film series includes the titles *First Contact*, *Generations* and *The Wrath of Khan*?

7 What kind of animal does Homer adopt as his new pet in the 2007 film *The Simpsons Movie*?

Half-time teaser

For an extra point, who can say 'toy boat' as fast as they can ten times without making a mistake?

Round 3: Behind Bars

1 In which country was the mysterious Man in the Iron Mask kept a prisoner for many years?

2 What was the name of the Paris prison stormed at the start of the French Revolution?

3 Which German was the last person imprisoned in the Tower of London?

4 Princetown in Devon is the location of which infamous British prison?

5 What was the name of the convict played by Ronnie Barker in *Porridge*?

6 Which Charles Dickens novel features an escaped convict called Magwitch?

7 In prison slang, what is a 'shake-down'?

Round 4: Pot Luck

1 Which king established the Church of England?

2 The active volcano Vesuvius overlooks which big Italian city?

3 Which US president was formerly a well-known movie actor?

4 What is the national currency of Turkey called?

5 What is a *faux pas* – a stepfather, a social blunder or a false ceiling?

6 If a South African offered you biltong would you drink it, eat it or put it in your wallet?

7 Which player takes the middle place in the front row of a rugby union scrum?

Jackpot

The heir to the British throne is traditionally made Prince of England, Prince of Scotland or Prince of Wales?

✴ Though filmed in director Peter Jackson's homeland New Zealand, J. R. R. Tolkien's original novel was inspired by places close to his Birmingham home. The Shire was based on what is now part of the Hall Green area of Birmingham, while the Two Towers were inspired by a tower folly and a waterworks tower in Ladywood, Birmingham.

Quiz 85

Round 1: Pot Luck

1 Which fictional hero starred in *A View to a Kill* and *The World Is Not Enough*?

2 The Sahara desert is getting smaller each year – true or false?

3 Which Victorian prime minister was called the Grand Old Man?

4 In which war did the Battle of the Atlantic take place?

5 What financial collapse of 1929 triggered the Depression of the 1930s?

6 Who were allowed to take part in track-and-field events in the Olympics for the first time in 1928?

7 What would you do with a pair of castanets – wear them, play them or keep them in a cage?

Round 2: Kings of the Jungle

1 Which biblical character was cast into the lions' den?

2 How many huge bronze lions stand at the foot of Nelson's Column in Trafalgar Square?

3 In which sport are the British Isles represented by the Lions?

4 What is the name of George of the Jungle's girlfriend – Kate, Griselda or Ursula?

5 Which of the following wrote songs for *The Lion King* – Elvis Presley, Paul McCartney or Elton John?

6 Which lion-related classic begins 'Once there were four children whose names were Peter, Susan, Edmund and Lucy'?

7 In which book did a Cowardly Lion go in search of courage?

Half-time teaser

For an extra point, what is 238 plus 22 minus 7?

Round 3: Fancy Food

1 Which of the following is not a TV chef – Nigel Slater, Nigella Lawson or Nigel Mansell?

2 Which cut of beef was supposedly knighted by an English king?

3 What, on a French menu, is the *plat du jour*?

4 What is the main ingredient of guacamole?

5 What might one find inside a profiterole?

6 Which country does moussaka come from?

7 What is Harry Ramsden famous for selling?

Round 4: Pot Luck

1 Which country does most of the world's gold come from?

2 Which famous British artist had the initials J. M. W. T.?

3 The African National Congress is a political party in which country?

4 Which of the following is not a type of wood – ebony, agony or mahogany?

5 What is a hollyhock – a wine, a small horse or a flower?

6 Which bird is noted for its tuneful song – the nightingale, the penguin or the vulture?

7 How many times have England won football's World Cup?

Jackpot

Which of the following jobs did Clint Eastwood not do for a time before taking up acting – firefighter, dancer or gas station attendant? ✳

✳ Sergio Leone, the director of some of Eastwood's most iconic movies, once said of his star, 'I like Clint Eastwood because he has only two facial expressions: one with the hat, and one without it.'

Quiz 86

Round 1: Pot Luck

1 How many centimetres are there in half a metre?

2 Which of the following creatures lay eggs – kangaroos, badgers or alligators?

3 What is a pistachio – a type of pasta, a ski slope or an edible nut?

4 The Royal Marines are part of which of the armed services – the army, the navy or the air force?

5 Mossad is an intelligence agency run by which state?

6 Which fictional elephant has a wife called Celeste and a rhinoceros enemy called King Rataxes?

7 What comes in basmati, pilau and wild varieties?

Round 2: Body Bits

1 How many kidneys do human beings have?

2 Which is the largest internal organ in the human body?

3 Where in the body might one find a lunula?

4 Whereabouts in the body is the thyroid gland?

5 How many chambers are there in a cow's stomach?

6 What does a chiropodist specialise in?

7 Where are the sinuses located?

Half-time teaser

For an extra point, who can list the most kings and queens of the UK since Victoria?

Round 3: House and Home

1 Which artist painted the ceiling of the Sistine Chapel?

2 What come in French, sash and bay varieties?

3 What name was given to the central structure in a medieval castle?

4 Which US state is home to Mark Twain's Tom Sawyer?

5 Which crustacean makes its home in the discarded shells of other sea creatures?

6 What is the name of the British prime minister's official country residence?

7 Manderley is the setting for which classic English novel? ✶

Round 4: Pot Luck

1 What colour are the clubs in a deck of cards?

2 Which of the following is not a real animal – a tiger moth, a tiger rat or a tiger shark?

3 Upon the banks of which river does Nottingham stand?

4 How does Tolstoy's Anna Karenina die?

5 What is an azalea – a bird, a deer or a plant?

6 In which country might you find a mountainous region called the Tyrol?

7 What do crossed swords on a map indicate?

Jackpot

Which of the following US states is not on the east coast – California, Florida or New York?

✶ Manderley was loosely based on a real building, called Menabilly, in Cornwall. Such was the success of the novel that Manderley became for a time the most common house name in the UK.

Quiz 87

Round 1: Pot Luck

1 In the nursery rhyme, where should one go to see a fine lady upon a white horse?

2 What colour is the cross on the Swiss national flag?

3 What is the French town of Cognac famous for?

4 Who, in 2000, was chosen to be presenter of television's *Big Brother*?

5 Who delayed fighting the Spanish until he had finished his game of bowls? ✳

6 What is the British equivalent of an American realtor?

7 Which animal comes in Javan, Sumatran and white varieties?

Round 2: Ships Away

1 What was the name of Nelson's flagship at the Battle of Trafalgar?

2 What kind of vessel has a conning tower?

3 What is the name of the clipper ship badly damaged by fire in London in 2007?

4 What name was given to the stones formerly placed at the bottom of the hull below the cargo hold to keep a ship steady?

5 What name is given to the inky patterns many sailors have pricked into their skin?

6 What, on a galleon, was a spanker?

7 Which World War II cruiser is now moored as a museum in the River Thames?

Half-time teaser

For an extra point, who can make up the funniest name for a new vegetable?

Round 3: Days of the Week

1 Upon which day of the week does Easter Day always fall?

2 Which Christian season begins on Ash Wednesday?

3 Which is the most common day of the week for heart attacks?

4 Which is the only day of the week named after a Roman god?

5 What is Wednesday called in French?

6 On which day does the Queen annually give out gifts of money to a small number of select subjects?

7 Which day is considered especially unlucky when it coincides with the thirteenth day of the month?

Round 4: Pot Luck

1 What is a large group of insects called?

2 What kind of animal is a beagle – a bird of prey, a dog or a small bee?

3 In which ball game is the playing area limited by tramlines?

4 Which war cost the most US lives – the US Civil War, World War II or the Vietnam War?

5 What was the name of King Arthur's queen?

6 What are cumulus and nimbus examples of?

7 Which two colours are the stripes on the Cat in the Hat's hat?

Jackpot

Male followers of which religion wear turbans – Hindus, Sikhs or Buddhists?

＊Unfortunately, no eyewitness account of this story survives. In reality, the delay in setting sail probably owed more to adverse winds and currents.

Quiz 88

Round 1: Pot Luck

1 What kind of creature goes 'gobble-gobble-gobble'?

2 Alongside Dutch and German, which is the third official language in Belgium?

3 With which of the following writers is Dorset associated – Sir Walter Scott, Thomas Hardy or John Milton?

4 What is an aphid – an insect, a fish or a snake?

5 In which country is sumo wrestling a national sport?

6 Which character in *Alice in Wonderland* fades until all that is left is its smile?

7 How much money do you have in your hand if you are holding a pony?

Round 2: Identity Parade

1 Which English queen was referred to as Good Queen Bess?

2 Which Scottish football club are known as the Bhoys?

3 Which great jazz musician had the nickname Satchmo?

4 What was Mickey Mouse's original name?

5 What is Sean Connery's real first name – Bill, Thomas or Spike?

6 Which US president was known as Ike?

7 In fiction, what is the secret identity of Sir Percy Blakeney?

Half-time teaser

For an extra point, who, in one minute, can list the most animals beginning with the letter B?

Round 3: Third Time Lucky

1 What are 'the three R's'?

2 Which churchman was the deadly enemy of the Three Musketeers?

3 Who reigned last – Edward III, George III or Henry III?

4 Which are more serious – first-degree burns or third-degree burns?

5 Which of the following was a dinosaur with three horns – a triceratops, a trilobite or a troglodyte?

6 Which country gave birth to the short-lived Third Reich?

7 What is 333 plus 333 minus 33?

Round 4: Pot Luck

1 Which nursery rhyme character met a pieman going to the fair?

2 What is Burkina Faso – the name of an Italian sports car, an African country or a skimpy kind of beachwear?

3 Which pantomime character turned again on Highgate Hill?

4 In which sport is the Stanley Cup contested?

5 What is volume measured in – metres, square metres or cubic metres?

6 Of which country is Tallinn the capital?

7 What is a speedwell – a motorbike, a flower or a surfboard?

Jackpot

What is the maximum number of clubs a golfer is allowed to take with him during a round – ten, twelve or fourteen?

✳ It is not certain where Lewis Carroll got the idea of his grinning, disappearing character from, but it has been suggested he may have been inspired by a popular type of cheese, which was moulded into the form of the animal in question. People who bought the cheese ate it from the creature's tail upwards, until all that was left was its face.

Quiz 89

Round 1: Pot Luck

1 What was the name of the family who took in Paddington Bear?

2 Which two colours look the same to most colour-blind people?

3 Which football team plays at the Stadium of Light in Lisbon?

4 Which part of the UK is governed from Stormont?

5 Jacaranda, larch and teak are all species of what?

6 Which Indian leader was assassinated in 1948?

7 What is the secret identity of Don Diego de la Vega?

Round 2: Spaced Out

1 What kind of star is also known as a meteor?

2 Which royal appointment has been held by John Flamsteed, Edmond Halley and Martin Rees?

3 What is Andromeda – a star, a planet or a galaxy?

4 Which planet in the solar system is nearest to the Sun?

5 The Sun is 330 times larger than the Earth – true or false?

6 Which cartoon series stars New York pizza delivery boy Philip Fry?

7 By what other name is the Pole Star or North Star known?

Half-time teaser

For the youngest member of each team: For an extra point, who can name three numbers that begin with the letter T?

Round 3: Things People Say

1 According to the proverb, what does one swallow not make?

2 If someone is two sandwiches short of a picnic what are they?

3 According to the slogan, coughs and sneezes spread what?

4 What does the Latin phrase *caveat emptor* mean?

5 According to the proverb, what should you save your breath for?

6 Which television quiz produced the phrase 'I've started, so I'll finish'?

7 According to Dr Samuel Johnson, when two Englishmen meet their talk is always of – what?

Round 4: Pot Luck

1 Which fruit recently overtook the apple as Britain's favourite?

2 Which bird comes in bull, green and zebra varieties?

3 54 per cent of Asia is covered by what – water, mountains or desert?

4 What colour are the flowers of lily of the valley?

5 A polar bear can run faster than a reindeer – true or false?

6 According to the Bible, on which mountain did Noah's Ark come to rest? ✳

7 What would you do with a knickerbocker glory – wear it, drink it or eat it?

Jackpot

How old was Mozart when he died – thirty-six, forty-six or fifty-six?

✳Various claims have been made over the years concerning the Ark's final resting place and several photographs taken from high altitude apparently show inexplicable boat-like remains on remote mountain summits. None of these have, however, been confirmed to date.

Quiz 90

Round 1: Pot Luck

1 It has never snowed in the Sahara – true or false?

2 What name is given to the bony structures that grow from the heads of deer?

3 In which television soap opera do the Baldwin and Battersby families feature?

4 Some sharks lay eggs – true or false?

5 What was the name of Elizabeth II's sister?

6 In which country is Farsi the official language?

7 Which kind of animal can have up to 300 pairs of ribs?

Round 2: Mythical Monsters

1 What kind of monster is St George supposed to have killed?

2 On which Greek island did King Minos keep the Minotaur?

3 Which mythical creature appears on the royal coat of arms?

4 Which English hero battled with Grendel and Grendel's monstrous mother?

5 Which inhabitant of the sea is said to have the top half of a woman and the bottom half of a fish?

6 In ancient myth, what kind of creature was the terrifying Roc?

7 Which creature of Irish folklore screams to warn the living of approaching death?

Half-time teaser

For an extra point, who can repeat the tongue-twister 'Peter Piper picked a peck of pickled peppers' three times quickly without making a mistake?

Round 3: Law and Order

1 What is the name of the policeman in the Noddy books?

2 How were condemned criminals executed at Tyburn?

3 Which British TV detective drama was set on the island of Jersey?

4 Which fictional amphibian was taken to court for driving recklessly in his new car?

5 What is a modern policeman's stick or club called?

6 What is the popular name of the Royal Canadian Mounted Police?

7 Which of the following is an informal name for a policeman – Nobby, Bobby or Robbie?

Round 4: Pot Luck

1 Which film hero shares a first name with that of a US state? ⁎

2 Which is furthest south – Essex, Surrey or Hampshire?

3 What were the Marx Brothers famous as – comedians, philosophers or clothing manufacturers?

4 In which European city did Anne Frank hide with her family from invading Nazis?

5 Where might one find a bolster?

6 On how many hills was Rome built?

7 In which month are hares said to go mad?

Jackpot

Which Apollo mission was crewed by James Lovell, Jack Swigert and Fred Haise – 9, 11 or 13?

⁎ It is explained on screen at one point that the hero's real name is Henry, and that he borrowed his more famous name from that of the family dog.

Quiz 91

Round 1: Pot Luck

1 In which film saga is Princess Leia a character?

2 What is a group of monkeys called?

3 Which country was ruled by the Taliban from 1996 to 2001?

4 What might you find in a vespiary?

5 What is hydrophobia the fear of?

6 Which Wayne remains to date the youngest player ever to score for England's national football team?

7 Where might you apply mascara – to your teeth, your eyes or your toes?

Round 2: Urban Sprawl

1 Which Welsh city became capital of Wales in 1955?

2 Which is the largest city in Africa?

3 Which of the following is not a town in the USA – Boring, Odd or Splatt?

4 Which is further north – Liverpool or Manchester?

5 The Irish town of Waterford is famous for which product?

6 Which is the only city that is located in more than one continent?

7 Which is the largest city in California?

Half-time teaser

For an extra point, who can perform the most perfect drumroll with their hands?

Round 3: Supporting Casts

1 Which ancient Greek god is depicted supporting the world on his shoulders?

2 What is the name of Bertie Wooster's manservant?

3 Who had a loyal Scottish servant called John Brown?

4 Who filled the role of deputy prime minister under Tony Blair?

5 In the novels of Terry Pratchett, Discworld rests on four elephants standing upon what?

6 What was the name of Phileas Fogg's manservant in the Jules Verne novel *Around the World in Eighty Days*?

7 Which superhero has a butler called Alfred?

Round 4: Pot Luck

1 What is the art of making sculptures out of folded paper called?

2 What, according to the writer Edward Bulwer-Lytton, is mightier than the sword?

3 What did the S in the name of US President Harry S. Truman stand for?

4 How many points is a maximum break in snooker?

5 With which foodstuff is the Cambridgeshire village of Stilton connected? *

6 Which famous commander observed that an army marches on its stomach?

7 How many women have walked on the Moon?

Jackpot

The weight of an adult blue whale is equivalent to that of how many people – 180, 1800 or 18,000?

✳ Stilton may have given its name to the foodstuff in question, but it is no longer made there. Today, by law, the name can only be applied to the product when produced in the counties of Derbyshire, Leicestershire and Nottinghamshire. Thus, today, even if it is actually made in Stilton itself, the product cannot be sold under the Stilton name.

Quiz 92

Round 1: Pot Luck

1 What is a Portuguese man o' war?

2 What were William's gang in the *Just William* books called?

3 Which comedy series featured characters called Edina, Patsy and Bubble?

4 Which was the first country to send a man into space?

5 What is the name given to the grassland that covers 40 per cent of Africa?

6 What do the initials UXB stand for?

7 What kind of story typically begins with the line 'Once upon a time'?

Round 2: Two by Two

1 Which two colours make orange when mixed?

2 Which national football team was the first to win two successive World Cup titles?

3 Which sign of the zodiac is represented by a pair of scales?

4 What is the name of the bowler-hatted twins in the *Tintin* stories?

5 How many people did Jesus feed with two fish?

6 Of which country was Constantine II the last king?

7 If three are a crowd, what are two?

Half-time teaser

For an extra point, who can be first to identify the lowest number that can be divided exactly by both 3 and 4?

Round 3: Little Critters

1 Which kind of animal inspired Robert the Bruce to try again? ✶

2 Which creature comes in goliath, stag and diving varieties?

3 Which insects do you have in your pants if you are restless or jittery?

4 Which small creatures do aardvarks eat – worms, termites or flies?

5 Which insect is known for its prayer-like stance?

6 Which small creature kills ten times as many Mexicans with its sting as snakes do with their bite?

7 Not all bees can sting – true or false?

Round 4: Pot Luck

1 Which colour is called *jaune* in French?

2 After Christmas, on which special day are the most greetings cards received?

3 Which car manufacturer makes the Accord, the Civic and the Prelude?

4 What, according to showman P. T. Barnum, is born every minute?

5 What is 999 minus 9 minus 9?

6 Who was the creator of The Muppets?

7 Where does dawn occur first – York or New York?

Jackpot

How long did it take Handel to write his Messiah – twenty-four days, twenty-four months or twenty-four years?

✶ Sadly, this legend may not be based on historical truth, as it does not appear in connection with Robert the Bruce before the nineteenth century. Perhaps significantly, similar tales are told about other historical figures, as far back as the Mongolian leader Tamerlane and the Jewish king David.

Quiz 93

Round 1: Pot Luck

1 Only female ducks quack – true or false?

2 Which is the only US state that begins with the letter G?

3 Morse Code relied upon the use of dots and – what?

4 What is a surgeon's knife called?

5 What two colours does willow-pattern china traditionally come in?

6 Who famously painted his grandson blowing bubbles?

7 What is the H in H_2O?

Round 2: Doctors' Orders

1 For what discovery is Scottish scientist Sir Alexander Fleming remembered?

2 Which deadly disease was officially eradicated around the world in 1980?

3 How do you spell 'measles'?

4 Where was acupuncture first developed – Japan, China or Africa?

5 What is myopia otherwise known as?

6 What is *mal de mer*?

7 Which part of the body is affected by cataracts?

Half-time teaser

For an extra point, who can make the most words of two or more letters out of 'reasonable'?

Round 3: Leaders of the Pack

1 What is the leader of a Cub Scout troop called?

2 Which leader was famous for writing a little red book?

3 Of which African nation was Idi Amin dictator?

4 Who led the Mongol hordes who overran Asia in the early thirteenth century?

5 Which British prime minister was the target of a bomb attack in Brighton in 1984?

6 Which Soviet leader was called 'Uncle Joe'?

7 What title is given to the leader of a group of Brownies?

Round 4: Pot Luck

1 According to the proverb, what never won fair lady?

2 Which car manufacturer makes the Camargue, the Corniche and the Phantom?

3 Which children's news programme has been presented over the years by, among others, John Craven, Juliet Morris and Ellie Crisell?

4 Is a metronome used by artists, musicians or sculptors?

5 What colour eyes does an albino animal have?

6 In which Beijing square were protesting students massacred in 1989?

7 What kind of creature is a marlin – a bird of prey, a stoat or a fish?

Jackpot

How many people are born on average every minute around the world – 10, 100 or 1000?

✻ The details of willow-pattern china tell the story of a pair of lovers who elope together across a bridge pursued by the girl's disapproving father. The origins of the legend are uncertain, but are probably English rather than Chinese.

Quiz 94

Round 1: Pot Luck

1 What colour is Worcestershire sauce?

2 Whereabouts in the world is Hudson Bay?

3 Which comedian wanted to know the way to Amarillo in 2005?

4 Which football team is nicknamed the Cobblers?

5 In medicine, what do the initials GP stand for?

6 By what name was boxer Muhammad Ali originally known?

7 In which country was the television comedy *'Allo 'Allo* set?

Round 2: Tools of the Trade

1 What was the name of the short sword used by pirates and other contemporary seafarers?

2 What is an auctioneer's hammer called?

3 Who carries a crozier?

4 Who might use a Sussex trug?

5 Which two tools formed the emblem of Soviet Russia?

6 Who might make use of lures, reels and floats?

7 Who uses an anvil to do their work? *

Half-time teaser

For an extra point, who can toss heads on a coin three times in the fewest throws?

Round 3: Holiday Destinations

1 Where is the Algarve holiday region?

2 Where was Europe's first Disney resort opened in 1992?

3 Malibu is a beach resort in which country – Australia, the USA or South Africa?

4 In which ocean are the islands of the Maldives?

5 Which European country attracts the most international tourists?

6 On which Scottish estate does Elizabeth II spend much of the summer?

7 Which holiday destination includes among its attractions the Tower, the Pleasure Beach and the Golden Mile?

Round 4: Pot Luck

1 Where is the Millennium Stadium located?

2 The word 'smog' is a combination of which two words?

3 What is a claymore?

4 Who wrote the 'Moonlight Sonata'?

5 Which pop star's real name is Georgios Kyriacos Panayiotou?

6 Which letter is unpronounced in the word 'island'?

7 How many pounds are there in 'a grand'?

Jackpot

Which of the following has not played Dr Who – David Tennant, Christopher Eccleston or Ewan McGregor?

✳Anvils were once considered magical objects. Sick children were sometimes laid on an anvil in the belief that this would cure them or their ailment.

Quiz 95

Round 1: Pot Luck

1 Which country lies east of Portugal?

2 What would you do with an enchilada – eat it, drive it or keep it as a pet?

3 'May the Force be with you' is a quote from which film series?

4 Which crime writer has the real name Phyllis Dorothy James White?

5 The Channel Tunnel starts near which British port?

6 Who was the first British driver to win the Formula One title – Graham Hill, Mike Hawthorn or Jim Clark?

7 In the nursery rhyme, what did Georgie Porgie do to the girls that made them cry?

Round 2: Winners and Losers

1 Can you complete the proverb 'The bigger they come, – '?

2 What was the name of the giant killed by David?

3 Which is the only country apart from Brazil to have won more than three World Cups?

4 Which Greek hero tried unsuccessfully to rescue Eurydice from the Underworld?

5 Which English king defeated the French at Agincourt in 1415?

6 Which Conservative leader lost a general election to Labour in 2005?

7 Which international aid organisation has won the Nobel Peace Prize three times?

Half-time teaser

For an extra point, in two minutes, who can list the most words containing a double letter O?

Round 3: Bells and Whistles

1 Which famous bell is housed in St Stephen's Tower at the Houses of Parliament?

2 Where might you hear a bosun's whistle?

3 Who went down the mine singing 'Whistle while you work?'

4 Which Bell is credited with inventing the telephone?

5 What did football referees wave to attract the attention of players before the introduction of whistles in the 1880s?

6 Who, in the 1944 film *To Have and Have Not*, asked Humphrey Bogart if he could whistle?

7 People born within the sound of the bells of St Mary-le-Bow are known as what?

Round 4: Pot Luck

1 Who is the presenter of television's *The Weakest Link*?

2 The *Mauretania* was sister ship to which other famous but ill-fated vessel?

3 In which part of the world is Margaret Thatcher Day celebrated?

4 Which fellow tennis star did Andre Agassi marry in 2000?

5 Which television detective series features Detective Chief Inspector Tom Barnaby?

6 Where is a person's jugular vein?

7 From which sport comes the phrase 'hit for six'?

Jackpot

Including Pope Benedict XVI, how many popes have there been – 165, 265 or 1165?

✴Georgie Porgie was based upon George Villiers, 1st Duke of Buckingham, who was notorious for his many love affairs. Most scandalous of all was his friendship with the queen of France, which later formed the background for the novel *The Three Musketeers*.

Quiz 96

Round 1: Pot Luck

1 What, in pre-decimal coinage, was a tanner?

2 Which language gave English the words fjord, lemming and ski?

3 What does the I stand for in FBI?

4 In which television soap opera do the Butcher and Slater families feature?

5 If a person writes SWALK on an envelope containing a love letter, what does it mean?

6 Which two words were combined to create the new word 'blog'?

7 What are ordinary, non-wizard humans called in the Harry Potter books?

Round 2: Festive Frolics

1 With which festival might one associate the phrase 'trick or treat'?

2 Who wrote the Christmas favourite *The Snowman*?

3 Eggs, rabbits and baby animals are symbols of which Christian festival?

4 What name is given in many Spanish-speaking countries to the festival known elsewhere as Shrove Tuesday?

5 Which festival of Indian origin is otherwise known as 'The Festival of Lights'?

6 How many gifts are given in total in the song 'The Twelve Days of Christmas'?

7 Which day of the year is traditionally marked by morris and maypole dancing?

Half-time teaser

For an extra point, can you place the following James Bond actors in the order in which they first took on the role – Daniel Craig, Roger Moore, Pierce Brosnan, Timothy Dalton, Sean Connery?

Round 3: Eco Issues

1 Which gas is responsible for the greenhouse effect?

2 What kind of creature is threatening the destruction of Australia's Great Barrier Reef?

3 Which huge South American rainforest is shrinking in size each year, threatening widespread climate change?

4 Which fish, declining in numbers, caused a war between Iceland and the UK in 1975?

5 What term describes a car that is powered by more than one kind of fuel?

6 Where do gorillas live in the wild – in deserts, marshes or forests?

7 Which is the world's busiest international passenger airport?

Round 4: Pot Luck

1 What is the correct spelling of 'receive'?

2 What is the correct term for the cry of a peacock – a coo, a squeak or a scream?

3 With what do you associate the brand name Moët et Chandon?

4 Which letter is not pronounced in 'knock'?

5 Which kind of animal comes in horseshoe, pipistrelle and vampire varieties?

6 What were used as balls in the game of croquet played in *Alice in Wonderland*?

7 In Australian slang, what is a 'sheila'? ✳

Jackpot

Which modern capital was formerly known as Edo – Shanghai, Beijing or Tokyo?

✳ Other colourful examples of Australian slang include 'ripper' (great), 'tinny' (can of beer), 'dinkum' (good) and 'bush telly' (campfire).

Quiz 97

Round 1: Pot Luck

1 What is a large group of fish called?

2 Which is the missing Teletubby – Dipsy, Laa Laa, Tinky Winky and – ?

3 Under what name did Volgograd experience severe fighting during World War II?

4 What comes in marram, sedge and rye varieties?

5 Which Spanish city is notable for its unfinished cathedral designed by Antoni Gaudi? +

6 How many locks are there on the Suez Canal?

7 In text messaging, what does PLS stand for?

Round 2: Time

1 How many minutes are there in two and a half hours?

2 What do the initials GMT stand for?

3 Who wrote the best-selling *A Brief History of Time*?

4 Who, in 1964, noted that the times they are a-changing?

5 What bird-related timepiece was first made in the Black Forest?

6 There are no clocks in Las Vegas gambling casinos – true or false?

7 Which age came before the Bronze Age?

Half-time teaser

For an extra point, can you name a country whose name contains the letter Q?

Round 3: Black and Blue

1 Which blue creature is the world's largest living mammal?

2 Who released a best-selling album in 2006 called *Back to Black*?

3 From which part of the UK did the regiment known as the Black Watch come?

4 Which artist had a Blue Period between 1901 and 1904?

5 Which black-coloured animals are considered lucky?

6 Members of which of the UK's armed forces traditionally wear a dark blue uniform?

7 What, in astronomy, results from a collapsed star?

Round 4: Pot Luck

1 What is the main colour of a five-pound note?

2 Male followers of which religion wear a yarmulke or kippah?

3 Which US president once admitted to cutting down a cherry tree with his hatchet?

4 Colombo is the capital of which country?

5 Which popular high street chain store was founded by Terence Conran?

6 Which film actor is nicknamed 'The Muscles from Brussels'?

7 What is chervil – a variety of sausagemeat, a type of cheese or a herb?

Jackpot

How many gates does the Thames Barrier have – ten, twelve or sixteen?

✳Gaudí's designs astonished his contemporaries. Even at the start of his career, when he was awarded his qualification as an architect, one of his teachers observed, 'Who knows if we have given this diploma to a nut or to a genius. Time will tell.'

Quiz 98

Round 1: Pot Luck

1 In the nursery rhyme, how many bags of wool did the black sheep have in total?

2 What kind of a creature is a roadrunner?

3 How many people are there in a polo team – four, six or eight?

4 Which language provided English with the words bonanza, siesta and tornado?

5 Which Charles Dickens novel has a hero called Philip Pirrip?

6 With which city is a faithful dog called Greyfriars Bobby associated?

7 Which fictional character slept right through the American War of Independence?

Round 2: Signs and Symbols

1 What is the national emblem of Canada?

2 What is the emblem of the conservation organisation the WWF?

3 What was the symbol of the German Nazi party called?

4 Which shape are most warning signs on British roads – circular, triangular or rectangular?

5 Which animal is the emblem of Tottenham Hotspur football club?

6 What is indicated by a letter c contained in a circle?

7 Which vegetable is a national emblem of Wales? ✳

Half-time teaser

For an extra point, who can spell 'chihuahua'?

Round 3: Crazy Creatures

1 What kind of animal is a pug – a fish, a dog or a badger?

2 Which venomous animal has a bill like a duck, a tail like a beaver and lays eggs?

3 Which pink-coloured bird, for unknown reasons, often stands on just one leg?

4 What type of animal are loons and potoos?

5 The ocelot is a member of which family – cats, dogs or monkeys?

6 Is the bongo a species of snake, lizard or antelope?

7 Which bird is said to hide its head in the sand if danger approaches?

Round 4: Pot Luck

1 Which kinds of creature belong to the order Lepidoptera?

2 With which sea is the Wash connected?

3 How many brothers and sisters did Queen Victoria have – three, seven or none?

4 From which musical comes the song 'My name is Tallulah'?

5 Which is the odd one out – Newcastle, Berwick-upon-Tweed or Edinburgh?

6 What name is given to a person who supposedly turns into a wolf in the light of a full moon?

7 What colour is saffron?

Jackpot

Which of the following is the world's best-selling English-language daily newspaper – *The Times,* the *New York Times* or the *Sun*?

✻The vegetable in question became the national emblem after it was supposedly worn by Welsh soldiers fighting under King Cadwallader to distinguish them from their Saxon enemies.

Quiz 99

Round 1: Pot Luck

1 Which country is commonly referred to as Down Under?

2 What did the Duke of Wellington refer to as 'the scum of the earth'?

3 What would you make in a samovar?

4 Which is 'the city that never sleeps'?

5 Which member of the onion family is said to repel vampires?

6 Which has more tines – a fork, a rake or a pitchfork?

7 What would you do with a kazoo – play it, stroke it or live in it?

Round 2: Name Games

1 Who was known as 'The Lady of the Lamp'?

2 Which city is also known as 'the Big Easy'?

3 Who was known as 'The Butcher of Baghdad'?

4 By what nickname are South Africa's rugby union team known?

5 Which cowboy actor was nicknamed 'The Duke'?

6 Which first name was used as a nickname for British soldiers fighting in World War I?

7 Which city is sometimes called 'the windy city'?

Half-time teaser

For the youngest member of each team: For an extra point, who, in one minute, can think up the most rhymes for the word 'mop'?

Round 3: Tourist Attractions

1 The pyramids of Giza are located close to which modern city?

2 Which city boasts among its sights the Brandenburg Gate?

3 On the banks of which river is the London Eye?

4 The Spanish Steps are a famous feature of which European city?

5 Which European city is well known for its Grand Canal?

6 The Eiffel Tower is the tallest structure in which European city?

7 Which world-famous tourist attraction opened in Anaheim, California, in 1955?

Round 4: Pot Luck

1 In which direction does a stalagmite grow – upwards or downwards?

2 What did the Suffragettes demand?

3 What in cockney rhyming slang is a 'Cain and Abel'?

4 Which is the odd one out – the boot, the screwdriver or the thumbscrew?

5 Which Scottish city featured in the title of several films starring a rugged Australian crocodile hunter?

6 What was the name of the Bogeyman created by Raymond Briggs?

7 Which breed of dog has Elizabeth II kept as pets for many years?

Jackpot

To which location did Thomas Cook arrange the first modern organised tourist excursion in 1841 – Bournemouth, Margate or Loughborough?

* The nickname refers to the refreshing breezes that blow across the city, although there have also been suggestions that it was originally inspired by the boasting of its inhabitants.

Quiz 100

Round 1: Pot Luck

1 What do bees collect to make honey?

2 Who was cinema's Terminator?

3 What does CND campaign against?

4 Which family of birds do choughs belong to? ✕

5 With which team did Bill Shankly spend most of his managerial career?

6 Who are trained at RADA?

7 James Herriot's *All Creatures Great and Small* was about the experiences of a country – what?

Round 2: Odd One Out

1 Which is the odd one out – the Himalayas, the Alps or the Fens?

2 Which of the following is the odd one out – *Alice's Adventures in Wonderland*, *Through the Looking-Glass* or *Swallows and Amazons*?

3 Who is the odd one out – Seamus Heaney, Ted Hughes or Damien Hurst?

4 Which of the following was not an Anglo-Saxon kingdom – Mercia, Macedonia or Wessex?

5 Which is the odd one out – Bolivia, Ghana or Guyana?

6 Which of the following is not a citrus fruit – a lemon, a grapefruit or an apple?

7 Which is the odd one out – barrister, chorister or solicitor?

Half-time teaser

For an extra point, who can name the most African countries?

QUIZZES 201

Round 3: Last Words

1 Who died with the last words 'Kiss me, Hardy' (or, possibly, 'Kismet, Hardy')?

2 Who said 'Et tu, Brute?' just before dying of stab wounds?

3 Which classic monster movie ends with the line 'Oh, no! It wasn't the airplanes. It was Beauty killed the Beast'?

4 Which English king's last words were 'Monks! Monks! Monks!'

5 Which film ends with the line 'Tomorrow is another day'?

6 Which composer died with the last words 'I shall hear in heaven'?

7 Which British monarch died with the last words 'Do not let poor Nelly starve'?

Round 4: Pot Luck

1 Which two colours feature in the Canadian flag?

2 Who wrote a novel about Emma Woodhouse?

3 Where might you find a pixel?

4 Which animals are the source of cashmere wool?

5 What is the subject matter of television's *Top Gear*?

6 Where did the ancient Romans go to see chariot races?

7 What colour is Thomas the Tank Engine?

Jackpot

What might be repaired on a wooden or metal last – a sword, a shoe or a ship?

✳ The soul of the legendary King Arthur is said to have passed into a chough when he died, hence the appearance of a chough in Cornwall's coat of arms. Unfortunately, the chough died out in Cornwall in the 1970s, but in 2001 a pair of choughs returned to Cornwall and managed to breed once more.

Quiz 1 for Grannies and Grandpas

Round 1: Pot Luck

1 The Siege of Ladysmith was a key event in which war?

2 Who danced in puddles in the film *Singin' in the Rain*?

3 Which of the following was not one of the Von Trapp children – Liesl, Kurt, Hans or Gretl?

4 Which classic TV series featured Napoleon Solo and Illya Kuryakin?

5 What might one secure with a Windsor knot?

6 In which Charles Dickens story is Ebenezer Scrooge a character?

7 In which year did the last horse-drawn taxi disappear from the streets of London – 1907, 1927 or 1947?

Round 2: The Royals

1 What royal title was bestowed upon Princess Anne in 1987?

2 How many children did Queen Anne have – eleven, seventeen or twenty-seven?

3 Which English king supposedly ordered the tide not to come in?

4 Who was the father of Elizabeth II?

5 Elizabeth II, Prince Charles and Prince William are all left-handed – true or false?

6 By what name did Bessie Wallis Warfield become better known?

7 In which year did Prince Charles marry Diana Spencer – 1978, 1981 or 1983?

Half-time teaser

For an extra point, who can do the best impression of either Marlene Dietrich or Winston Churchill?

Round 3: Battles of Britain

1 Which day inspired the 1962 film *The Longest Day*?

2 What was the first name of Winston Churchill's wife?

3 What was the codename given to the Normandy invasion?

4 Who was the leader of Italy's fascists during World War II?

5 What name was given to that part of France run by Marshal Pétain during World War II?

6 Who fought the Rockers on British beaches in the 1960s?

7 When did British and Argentinian forces fight for control of the Falklands – 1972, 1982 or 1992?

Round 4: Pot Luck

1 Of the Seven Wonders of the World, which are the only ones still standing?

2 Blunt, Burgess, Philby and Maclean became well-known as what – pop stars, writers or spies?

3 Which famous boxer died in an air crash in 1969?

4 Who presents the TV quiz show *Deal or No Deal*?

5 Which holds more – a pint bottle or a litre bottle?

6 Was a farthing a quarter of an old penny, half of an old penny or four old pennies?

7 According to the proverb, what can't you teach an old dog?

Jackpot

In which year did the wearing of seatbelts become compulsory in the UK – 1963, 1973 or 1983?

⋆Sadly, this story appears to have been a much later invention, dating from the twelfth century. It is thought possible that the idea of the king in question ruling the waves may actually have evolved from contemporary descriptions of him commanding the seas with his Viking fleets.

Quiz 2 for Grannies and Grandpas

Round 1: Pot Luck

1 Who was Bing Crosby's partner in *The Road to Morocco* and other *Road* films?

2 Where might one find a Lazy Susan – in the dining room, in the garden or in the street?

3 Which construction toy was invented by Frank Hornby in 1900?

4 Until 1957 no television programmes were broadcast between six and seven o'clock in the evening so parents could put children to bed – true or false?

5 Which was the first Beatles album title track to top the British singles charts?

6 Fred Perry was famous as what – a television gardener, a tennis player or a folk singer?

7 What mishap occurred during both the 1946 and 1947 FA Cup finals?

Round 2: The Rock 'n' Roll Era

1 Who was known as 'the Pelvis'?

2 Where, in the 1950s, might one have seen a duck's tail, other than on a duck?

3 Which 1950s musician was called the Man in Black?

4 What do the initials R&B stand for?

5 By what name did Harry Webb become well known?

6 When was the electric guitar invented – 1931, 1951 or 1971?

7 What was Elvis Presley's first UK number one hit single?

Half-time teaser

For an extra point, who can list the most prime ministers who have held office during the reign of Elizabeth II?

Round 3: Games People Play

1 Which game was invented first – Monopoly, Cluedo or Scrabble?

2 There are six weapons in Cluedo – a knife, a revolver, as lead pipe, a rope, a candlestick and what else?

3 Which colour moves first in chess?

4 In which century was the jigsaw puzzle invented – the seventeenth century, the eighteenth century or the nineteenth century?

5 Which is the most expensive property in Monopoly?

6 What is the American name for the game of draughts?

7 What number does the bingo call 'two fat ladies' refer to? *

Round 4: Pot Luck

1 How many winks is a person said to take when they have a nap?

2 Richard Whiteley was for many years presenter of which TV programme?

3 In which year was 'Ernie (the fastest milkman in the west)' the UK Christmas number one – 1966, 1971 or 1976?

4 Which domestic football club did Bobby Moore play for at the time England won the World Cup?

5 Which is shorter – a yard or a metre?

6 On which item of domestic machinery might one expect to see the Singer name?

7 Loss of memory is termed magnesia, amnesia or anaesthesia?

Jackpot

In which year did Rowntree's Fruit Gums first go on sale – 1843, 1893 or 1943?

* Some bingo calls are better known than others. The more imaginative ones include 'baby's done it' (for 2, after 'number twos'), 'doctor's orders' (9, possibly from the name of a pill) and 'two little ducks' (22, from the shape). Oddly enough, no one knows for sure the origin of 'Kelly's eye' (for 1).

Quiz 1 for Mums and Aunties

Round 1: Pot Luck

1 What was the name of the race of ferocious warrior women in Greek mythology?

2 Mrs Danvers is the brooding housekeeper in which romantic classic?

3 Which king lost his crown jewels in the Wash?

4 Anton Edelmann, Jean-Christophe Novelli and Robert Carrier are all what?

5 How many books in the Bible are named after women?

6 Who had friends called Ross, Monica, Phoebe, Rachel and Chandler?

7 Which British equivalent of Barbie disappeared from toy shops in 1997?

Round 2: Soaps

1 Which British soap opera is set in the fictional village of Beckindale?

2 In which year did *EastEnders* begin – 1981, 1985 or 1990?

3 What was the name of the *Neighbours* character played by Kylie Minogue?

4 What is the name of the village pub in *The Archers*?

5 Members of which rock band made appearances in *Coronation Street* in 2005?

6 Which former soap opera featured characters called Jimmy Corkhill and Sinbad?

7 In which soap opera is Tony Hutchinson the longest-running character?

Half-time teaser

For an extra point, who can draw the best picture of Marge Simpson?

Round 3: Soppy Stuff

1 How many lines are there in a sonnet?

2 Who wrote the 'Wedding March' often played at the end of marriage ceremonies?

3 What did my true love give to me on the third day of Christmas?

4 Which fictional character married Charles Hamilton, Frank Kennedy and Rhett Butler?

5 Which sculptor's most famous work shows two people kissing?

6 What romantic first was achieved by Norfolk woman Margery Brews on 14 February 1477?

7 How many years of marriage are celebrated on a diamond wedding anniversary?

Round 4: Pot Luck

1 With which product is the district of Bourneville particularly associated?

2 Who had hits in the 1970s with 'Hot love' and '20th century boy'?

3 Which heart-throb played the male lead in the 1965 film *Dr Zhivago*?

4 How long is a half in a professional football match, excluding extra time?

5 Which TV series had a central character called John Boy?

6 Where did the Bay City Rollers come from – California, Scotland or Australia?✳

7 Which brand of children's soft toys, featuring such characters as Quackers the Duck and Waddle the Penguin, was launched in 1994 and sparked an enduring collecting craze?

Jackpot

In which year was the paper plate invented – 1904, 1924 or 1944?

✳Members of the band are said to have chosen their name by throwing a dart at a map of the USA. The first throw landed on Arkansas, but concern about the pronunciation of the name persuaded them to throw a second dart, which landed on Bay City, Michigan.

Quiz 2 for Mums and Aunties

Round 1: Pot Luck

1 Which British city has a famous shopping centre called the Bull Ring?

2 What is the name of the concealing outer garment worn by many strict Muslim women?

3 When does a human develop fingerprints – before birth, by the age of two or by the age of nine?

4 In which year was 'Do they know it's Christmas?' the UK Christmas number one – 1981, 1984 or 1987?

5 In which children's book was Anne Shirley the central character?

6 Who wrote the poems on which the musical *Cats* was based?

7 What is the most common colour of a sapphire – red, green or blue?

Round 2: Cooking Up a Storm

1 What is calamari – octopus, squid or eel?

2 Which country was the original home of the Aga cooker?

3 What was cookery writer Delia Smith before she became a TV chef – a hairdresser, a dancer or a cleaner?

4 What is the main ingredient of hummus?

5 Which of the following is a herb – tarragon, paragon or harridan?

6 What are blutwurst, chorizo and mortadella varieties of?

7 What is the chief ingredient of scampi?

Half-time teaser

For an extra point, who can say 'I'd like a dozen bananas please' in the silliest voice?

Round 3: Trendy Togs

1 Which of the following is not a famous Italian fashion designer – Giorgio Armani, Juan Fangio or Guccio Gucci?

2 What is the Louis Vuitton company famous for producing?

3 With what product would one associate Jimmy Choo – shoes, handbags or skirts?

4 Who designed Diana Spencer's wedding dress in 1981?

5 In which sport do participants wear silks?

6 Which pop star has a daughter named Stella, who is a famous fashion designer?

7 Which is also an item of clothing – a python, a cobra or a boa?

Round 4: Pot Luck

1 On which finger of which hand is a wedding ring traditionally worn?＊

2 What name do Americans give to a baby's dummy?

3 According to the proverb, what shouldn't one put in one basket?

4 On which day are hot cross buns supposed to be eaten?

5 Which chain of cosmetics shops was founded by Anita Roddick in 1976?

6 What might a medieval woman do with a wimple – cook it, wear it or play it?

7 Which of the following is not an Indian dish – korma, carbonara or vindaloo?

Jackpot

According to Victorian etiquette, deceased husbands were mourned for two to three years – how long were deceased wives mourned for?

＊Ancient tradition insists that a vein leads directly from the finger in question to the heart. Custom further insists that a wedding ring should never be taken off; if this cannot be avoided it should be replaced as soon as possible, while repeating the marriage vows.

Quiz 1 for Dads and Uncles

Round 1: Pot Luck

1 Who flew Thunderbird 1?

2 With which rock group was Jim Morrison lead singer?

3 Which of the following did not play in the World Cup Final in 1966 –
Gordon Banks, Jimmy Greaves or Martin Peters?

4 In which year was the smoking ban introduced in England?

5 Which household tool incorporates bits and chucks?

6 Which classic TV sitcom was set in Grace Brothers department store?

7 What might one open with a worm?

Round 2: The Sporting Life

1 Which British football team play at the Stadium of Light?

2 What colour is the centre of the target in archery?

3 In which sport might a contestant employ a half-nelson?

4 With earnings of 122 million dollars, who was the highest paid sportsperson
of 2007?

5 How many people are there in a rugby league team?

6 How many times do riders go round the track in a speedway race?

7 In American football, what is the playing area called?

Half-time teaser

For an extra point, who can draw the best picture of US singer Dolly Parton?

Round 3: Oily Engines

1 Which car manufacturer makes the Brava, Ducato and Tipo?

2 Which of the following has an engine – a microlight, a hang-glider or a paraglider?

3 Which country used the T34 tank during World War II?

4 In which year did the Mini motor car make its first appearance – 1959, 1966 or 1969?

5 What colour was the three-wheeled vehicle featured in the TV series *Only Fools and Horses*? *

6 Which British island is famous for Tourist Trophy motorcycle racing?

7 Which car manufacturer made the cars driven by James Bond in *Goldfinger*, *Thunderball* and *Die Another Day*?

Round 4: Pot Luck

1 Which rock band was led by the ill-fated Kurt Cobain until 1994?

2 Who starred in the *Die Hard* movies?

3 Beside red and black, what is the third colour on a roulette wheel?

4 Which pop star's real name is David Robert Jones?

5 In which year were Scalextric model racing cars first produced – 1956, 1966 or 1976?

6 By what name was Captain Scarlet's deadly enemy Conrad Turner better known?

7 Which of the following magazines was founded by Hugh Hefner – *Country Life*, *Military Modelling* or *Playboy*?

Jackpot

In which year was Arthur Conan Doyle's *The Lost World* shown as the world's first in-flight movie – 1925, 1945 or 1965?

* The vehicle used in the series is often described as a Reliant Robin, but it is more correctly a Reliant Regal Supervan. One of the Supervans used in the series is now in the Cars of the Stars motor museum in Keswick, Cumbria. Another was sold in 2007 for £44,000.

Quiz 2 for Dads and Uncles

Round 1: Pot Luck

1 Which two Scottish football teams are known as 'The Old Firm'?

2 Of which band is Bono lead singer?

3 What were Destiny, Harmony, Melody, Rhapsody and Symphony called in *Captain Scarlet*?

4 Which of the Beatles died in 2001?

5 Which company claims that its products do 'exactly what it says on the tin'?

6 In which country was the longest tie ever made unveiled in 1995?

7 Which area east of Florida has a notorious reputation for the ships and aircraft that have disappeared there?

Round 2: The Reel Thing

1 Which was the first of the *Carry On* films – *Carry On Cowboy*, *Carry On Nurse* or *Carry On Sergeant*?

2 Which 1991 film had characters named after the colours white, orange, blue, blonde, pink and brown?

3 Who starred in *A Fistful of Dollars* and *For a Few Dollars More*?

4 Which film superhero's enemies include Oswald Cobblepot?

5 What was Red October in the 1990 film *The Hunt for Red October*?

6 Which war provided the historical setting for *Gone With the Wind*?

7 Which role was played by Michelle Pfeiffer in the 1992 film *Batman Returns*?

Half-time teaser

For an extra point who, in thirty seconds, can name the most British professional football teams beginning with the letter B?

Round 3: Down the Local

1 What is the name of the pub in *Coronation Street*?

2 Which brand of beer do John Mills and his companions look forward to drinking in the 1958 film *Ice Cold in Alex*?

3 What is the traditional drink of the Royal Navy?

4 Which English queen was known as Bloody Mary?

5 What is perry made from?

6 What kind of drink is Canada Dry?

7 When was the potato crisp invented – 1853, 1903 or 1953?

Round 4: Pot Luck

1 Which kind of shark caused terror in *Jaws* – a tiger shark, a blue shark or a great white shark?

2 Who was England's enemy during the Hundred Years' War?

3 Ermintrude was the name of a cow in which classic children's TV series?

4 Which national team won the first World Cup competition in 1930?

5 How many pairs of wings does a biplane have?

6 Members of which branch of the British Army are known as the Red Devils?

7 What was the name of the chief engineer on the original starship *Enterprise*?

Jackpot

When was the FA Cup founded – 1861, 1871 or 1881?

✳ According to one theory, the term dates back to the first match played between the two teams in question, in 1888. The two sets of players got on so well, according to one reporter at the time, that one could have believed they were all 'old firm friends'.

Quiz 1 for Teens

Round 1: Pot Luck

1 What is the name of the dog owned by the Simpson family in *The Simpsons*?

2 Which company advertises its products with the slogan 'Finger lickin' good'?

3 What do the initials GCSE stand for?

4 Whereabouts in the world was surfing invented?

5 Which of the following has venom in its tail – a rattlesnake, a stingray or a spider?

6 Which country won football's World Cup in 2006?

7 At which theme park can be found the Nemesis and Oblivion rides?

Round 2: Rock and Pop of the Noughties

1 Who is older – Kylie or Dannii Minogue?

2 What country of the UK do the pop group Franz Ferdinand come from?

3 Who smiled when her single topped the UK charts in July 2006?

4 Which Simon is a judge on the musical talent shows *The X Factor* and *Pop Idol*?

5 Who released his first solo album in 2002 with the title *Justified*?

6 Who sang about an 'American idiot' in 2004?

7 Which one of the following groups come from Wales – the Sugababes, the Stereophonics or the Hoosiers?

Half-time teaser

For an extra point, who can say the tongue-twister 'She sells seashells on the seashore' the most times without making a mistake?

Round 3: A Good Read

1 The 2005 film *The Chronicles of Narnia* was based on the C. S. Lewis book *The Lion, the Witch and the* – what? ✶

2 In which novel do Ralph and Piggy find themselves marooned with other schoolboys on a desert island?

3 What is the name of the house at Hogwarts in which Harry Potter is enrolled in the novels of J. K. Rowling?

4 In which novel is rebellious teenager Holden Caulfield the main character?

5 Who wrote a series of novels about trainee witch Tiffany Aching?

6 What was the name of the human farmer overthrown by the animals in *Animal Farm*?

7 Which 2003 novel by Christopher Paolini tells the story of a farm boy and his dragon Saphira?

Round 4: Pot Luck

1 Which of the following was not a composer – Beethoven, Rembrandt or Brahms?

2 What term describes a surfer falling off his board?

3 Who starred as the time-traveller Doctor Who when the series was revived in 2005?

4 What is the French word for 'nine'?

5 Which absorbs heat faster – black or white?

6 In which musical does a small boy ask for some more?

7 Where might you find the Great Red Spot?

Jackpot

How many years does the average modern Briton spend watching television in an average lifetime – three, eight or eleven?

✶Narnia may owe its name to the Italian town of Narni (called Narnia by the Romans) but in terms of its landscape it appears to have been modelled upon the wilder reaches of Northern Ireland, from which the author himself originally came, specifically County Down and the mountains of Mourne.

Quiz 2 for Teens

Round 1: Pot Luck

1 Krishna is a god in which religion?

2 Which sport involves making parachute jumps from clifftops, buildings or other high structures?

3 Which fictional hero had best friends called Sam, Pippin and Merry?

4 In rap slang, what is a 'homie'?

5 How many degrees are there in a circle?

6 What is 11.50 p.m. on a twenty-four-hour clock?

7 At what age can children in the UK legally end their schooling?

Round 2: Electronic Gizmos

1 Which company makes the PlayStation?

2 In text messaging, what do the initials GAL stand for?

3 Which item of computer equipment was originally known as an 'X–Y Position Indicator for a Display System'?

4 What do the initials CGI stand for?

5 In which year did Apple launch the iPod – 2001, 2004 or 2007?

6 What do the letters FAQ stand for?

7 Which video game series was criticised for glorifying car-stealing and other crimes?

Half-time teaser

For an extra point, who can stand on one leg for the longest period of time?

Round 3: A Trip to the Flicks

1 The first *Pirates of the Caribbean* film was subtitled *The Curse of the* – what?

2 In the 2002 film *Lilo & Stitch*, where does Lilo come from?

3 Which 2006 film told the story of a love affair between school basketball captain Troy Bolton and shy maths student Gabriella Montez?

4 What does Indy go in search of in the 2008 fourth Indiana Jones film?

5 Which 1995 film featured the Randy Newman song 'You've got a friend in me'?

6 What was the name of the heroine in the 2001 film subtitled *Tomb Raider*?

7 What was the name of the evil high priest in *The Mummy* and *The Mummy Returns*?

Round 4: Pot Luck

1 Most kinds of shark will drown if they stop swimming – true or false?

2 Which of the following numbers cannot be divided exactly by four – 16, 24 or 26?

3 Which Spanish football team plays at the Bernabeu Stadium?

4 What is the name of Death's apprentice in the novels of Terry Pratchett?

5 Which was larger – a velociraptor, a brachiosaurus or a tyrannosaurus rex?

6 Shakespeare does not mention the word 'lavatory' or 'toilet' even once in his plays – true or false?

7 Who wrote about Danny, the Champion of the World?

Jackpot

How many times will the average American visit a McDonald's during their lifetime – 180 times, 1800 times or 18,000 times?

✳ The iPod tradename was supposedly inspired by a line from the classic sci-fi movie *2001: A Space Odyssey*, in which a character delivers the order 'Open the pod bay door, Hal!'

Quiz 1 for Under-10s

Round 1: Pot Luck

1 If boys are made of frogs and snails and puppy dog tails, what are little girls made of?

2 What is the name of the big express train in the *Thomas the Tank Engine* stories?

3 How many centimetres are there in a metre?

4 On which day of the year is Bonfire Night celebrated?

5 What is a bluebottle?

6 Nelson's Column stands in the middle of which London square? ✳

7 A boy ate all but three of a packet of fifteen sweets – how many were left?

Round 2: Wild Animals

1 Which is larger – an eagle or an ostrich?

2 Which creatures make honey?

3 What stage does a frog go through between being frogspawn and an adult frog?

4 Which is the fastest land animal?

5 Which animal is the odd one out – Paddington, Winnie-the-Pooh, Bambi or Yogi?

6 Which wild animal is the tallest?

7 Not all snakes have a poisonous bite – true or false?

Half-time teaser

For an extra point, who can rub their tummy and pat their head at the same time?

Round 3: The Big Screen

1 What is the name of Shrek's wife?

2 In which film (and book) is Mowgli the central character?

3 Which 2001 film set in Monstropolis featured best friends Sulley and Mike?

4 What is the name of Mickey Mouse's girlfriend?

5 Which Disney film featured the song 'Under the sea'?

6 In which 2007 film do the Autobots battle with the Decepticons?

7 Which 2004 film included the characters Mr Incredible, Elastigirl and their children Violet, Daniel and Jack-Jack?

Round 4: Pot Luck

1 What is the opposite of 'inside'?

2 What is a young horse called?

3 Which is the nearest star to Earth?

4 What kind of animal was Beatrix Potter's Mrs Tiggywinkle?

5 How many sides does a rectangle have?

6 In the *Captain Underpants* books, how is Captain Underpants turned back into school principal Mr Krupp?

7 Who is Elizabeth II's husband?

Jackpot

Which of the following is not an event commonly included in contests for World's Strongest Man title – the Farmer's Walk, the Tip and Run or the Carry and Drag?

✴ Those who look closely at the statue will note that the famous admiral is depicted with an empty sleeve where his right arm was, but also that it lacks the familiar eye-patch that he is usually supposed to have worn after losing the sight in his right eye in battle in 1794. In fact, there is no evidence that Nelson ever wore an eyepatch, although he did sometimes wear an eyeshade against the glare of the sun.

Quiz 2 for Under-10s

Round 1: Pot Luck

1 How many minutes are there in an hour?

2 Which animal is famous for its quills?

3 How many months of the year have less than thirty days?

4 What is rain mixed with snow called?

5 Who might use a stethoscope?

6 What do vampire bats feed on?

7 Which fictional character has a best friend called Rude Ralph and enemies called Miss Battle-Axe and Great Aunt Greta?

Round 2: Around the World

1 What is the capital of France?

2 What is the world's highest mountain called? ✶

3 Which of the following is an island – Nicaragua, Jamaica or Belize?

4 Which of the world's oceans is the biggest?

5 Which US city is known as 'the Big Apple'?

6 The River Severn ends in the Bristol Channel – in which country of the UK does it begin?

7 Of which city is Hollywood a suburb?

Half-time teaser

For an extra point, who can hop on the spot twenty times without losing their balance?

Round 3: Fairy Tales and Nursery Rhymes

1 In the nursery rhyme, what did the knave of hearts steal?

2 What did the ugly duckling turn into?

3 How did the wolf destroy the houses of two of the Three Little Pigs?

4 In which folk tale does a giant say he can smell the blood of an Englishman?

5 Who finally managed to eat the Gingerbread Man?

6 Who got into the Three Bears' house and ate their porridge?

7 What did Jack break when he fell down the hill after Jill?

Round 4: Pot Luck

1 How many days are there in a week?

2 What is the motto of the Scout movement?

3 How many fives are there in thirty?

4 Which 1994 film featured the songs 'Can you feel the love tonight' and 'Circle of life'?

5 What is a sheep's coat called?

6 What is the usual colour of a daffodil?

7 What were the rulers of ancient Egypt called?

Jackpot

Which is extinct – the monitor lizard, the pterodactyl or the giant panda?

⚹Mountains are usually judged by their height above sea level, but there are other ways of measuring them. If they are measured from local ground level the highest mountain in the world is Nanga Parbat, in the Himalayas, which rises 7000 metres (22,966 feet) from its base to its summit.

Answers

Quiz 1 answers

Round 1

1 The prime minister. 2 Daniel Craig. 3 Australia. 4 A pumpkin.
5 Ireland. 6 Henry VIII. 7 Greenland.

Round 2

1 Pluto. 2 A wolf. 3 A colt. 4 Rodent. 5 Palomino (which is a horse – the others are breeds of pig). 6 The mammoth. 7 Rats.

Round 3

1 Dizzy. 2 *Blue Peter*. 3 Hal. 4 Scott Tracy. 5 *Grange Hill*. 6 *Spongebob Squarepants*. 7 *The Clangers*.

Round 4

1 They are exactly the same. 2 A grapefruit. 3 *The Lord of the Rings*. 4 Skin. 5 Mozart. 6 Italy. 7 Blue.

Jackpot 1463.

Quiz 2 answers

Round 1

1 WRIGGLE. 2 A cagoule. 3 Hirohito. 4 An outside toilet. 5 A cosmonaut.
6 Jealousy. 7 Sodor.

Round 2

1 The Sparrow. 2 Chicago. 3 Henry II. 4 Edinburgh. 5 Duncan.
6 John Lennon. 7 Dallas.

Round 3

1 Biology. 2 Sound. 3 Medicine. 4 France. 5 Oasis. 6 100 degrees.
7 *Rocket*.

Round 4

1 Thor. 2 A very large wave. 3 Canada. 4 *Top Gear*. 5 *Big Brother*. 6 True.
7 Amen.

Jackpot 1789.

Quiz 3 answers

Round 1

1 Wolves. **2** The Channel Islands. **3** A penguin. **4** Ambidextrous.
5 Popeye. **6** *The Angel of the North*. **7** Lady Jane Grey.

Round 2

1 Cricket. **2** Newcastle. **3** Ten. **4** Nottinghamshire. **5** Rally driving.
6 Fairground. **7** Edinburgh.

Round 3

1 The helicopter. **2** The Slinky. **3** True. **4** 1861. **5** The parachute.
6 Detect lies. **7** Microsoft.

Round 4

1 King Arthur. **2** Bigfoot. **3** Ruby. **4** Russia. **5** Kryptonite. **6** A mouse.
7 Amber.

Jackpot Two hours.

Quiz 4 answers

Round 1

1 True. 2 A ship. 3 Where a road crosses a railway.

4 A musical instrument. 5 Roald Amundsen. 6 A court. 7 Eels.

Round 2

1 Los Angeles. 2 Sheryl Crow. 3 *Home Alone*. 4 *The Lion King*.

5 Han Solo. 6 *King Kong*. 7 William Wallace.

Round 3

1 Northern Ireland. 2 Sherwood Forest. 3 1999. 4 Scotland.

5 Birmingham. 6 St Paul's. 7 East Anglia.

Round 4

1 Seaweed. 2 Q. 3 The hands and fingernails. 4 1988. 5 Mustard.

6 The bayonet. 7 Neville Chamberlain.

Jackpot 50 per cent.

Quiz 5 answers

Round 1

1 Buckingham Palace. 2 One quarter. 3 Mr Spock. 4 Seven.
5 The Tory party. 6 *Stingray*. 7 A fish.

Round 2

1 Butterflies. 2 Three pairs. 3 A caterpillar has around four times as many.
4 The Old Lady. 5 Its thorax. 6 A maggot. 7 True.

Round 3

1 The doctor. 2 A seed. 3 Cabbage. 4 Potatoes. 5 Bob Geldof. 6 Bananas.
7 Carrots.

Round 4

1 Marmalade. 2 Lady Godiva. 3 Dentists. 4 The Norman Conquest.
5 The dining room. 6 The Incas. 7 Green.

Jackpot 1963.

Quiz 6 answers

Round 1

1 Red, white and blue. 2 Quasimodo. 3 A hutch. 4 Blue. 5 A snake.
6 Elizabeth I. 7 Female.

Round 2

1 A black panther. 2 Himself or herself. 3 P. G. Wodehouse.

4 *Northern Lights* (by Philip Pullman). 5 *Horrible Histories*.

6 Leo Tolstoy. 7 *Five Children and It.*

Round 3

1 1820. 2 India. 3 On one's head. 4 A shirt. 5 Jackets. 6 Scotland.
7 Babies.

Round 4

1 St George. 2 St Paul's Cathedral. 3 Formula One motor-racing.

4 A cat. 5 The North Sea. 6 Argentina. 7 Botticelli.

Jackpot 1937.

Quiz 7 answers

Round 1

1 New York. 2 Two. 3 Holby. 4 Estonia. 5 Reading. 6 True. 7 Egypt.

Round 2

1 A squid. 2 Seals. 3 Water. 4 A small fish. 5 A tusk. 6 Five.
7 The *Flying Dutchman*.

Half-time teaser

Some possible answers are: Canada, Chad, Chile, Colombia, Congo.

Round 3

1 Britney Spears. 2 Rihanna (featuring Jay-Z). 3 Take That.
4 The electric guitar. 5 Leona Lewis. 6 Ann. 7 Madonna.

Round 4

1 Sherlock Holmes. 2 Juliet. 3 Elba. 4 A cob. 5 Rectangular. 6 Anglesey.
7 True.

Jackpot 1856.

Quiz 8 answers

Round 1

1 Sixty-four. 2 True. 3 An early bicycle. 4 Leeds. 5 A dry wind.
6 A mongoose. 7 Dutch elm disease.

Round 2

1 Blackbeard. 2 Long John Silver. 3 Johnny Depp. 4 The Jolly Roger.
5 Fifteen. 6 A gold coin. 7 It was eaten by a crocodile.

Round 3

1 True (separate bones in babies slowly fuse into single bones).
2 Adam and Eve. 3 The Flanders. 4 Oedipus. 5 Your aunt. 6 His mother.
7 They were first cousins.

Round 4

1 Popeye. 2 From the soil. 3 At Niagara. 4 Cliff Richard. 5 A toad.
6 Hardness. 7 Swiss.

Jackpot Five years.

Quiz 9 answers

Round 1

1 Black. 2 Belgian. 3 . Pennsylvania. 4 The town hall. 5 The navy.
6 The poppy. 7 Culloden.

Round 2

1 Richard I. 2 A dive-bomber. 3 London. 4 Everton. 5 Roundheads.
6 Detroit. 7 Louis XIV.

Round 3

1 True. 2 Iraq. 3 Tasmania. 4 Scotland. 5 Portugal and Spain.
6 Gauchos. 7 Easter Island (or Rapa Nui).

Round 4

1 Lava. 2 The Crown Jewels. 3 True. 4 An ace. 5 *Tirpitz*. 6 A dog.
7 Arrows.

Jackpot Twenty-two.

Quiz 10 answers

Round 1

1 Earthquakes. 2 Jess. 3 George Eliot. 4 Ireland. 5 *Top Cat* (also known in the UK as *Boss Cat*). 6 Coventry Cathedral. 7 The Red Devils.

Round 2

1 On Mount Olympus. 2 Odin. 3 Earth. 4 A theatre. 5 An elephant.
6 The Norse god Thor. 7 Mars.

Half-time teaser

One possible answer is: deinstitutionalisation, with twenty-two letters.

Round 3

1 Theseus. 2 Godzilla. 3 With its stare. 4 The Mysterons. 5 Loch Ness.
6 The abominable snowman. 7 *The Lord of the Rings*.

Round 4

1 India. 2 Black. 3 31 October. 4 Israel. 5 A rock stack in the Orkneys.
6 Antarctica. 7 Australia.

Jackpot Seven.

Quiz 11 answers

Round 1

1 Earthworms. 2 Badminton. 3 Ash. 4 David Beckham (in 2001).
5 The Battle of Hastings. 6 A synagogue. 7 True.

Round 2

1 Dick Turpin. 2 The west. 3 Harry Potter. 4 Sherlock Holmes.
5 The Campbells. 6 Spiderman. 7 Gremlins.

Round 3

1 Red. 2 Green. 3 A small bird. 4 Elton John (with 'Candle in the
wind '97'). 5 Yellow. 6 Washington, DC. 7 Red.

Round 4

1 The Vatican. 2 Its snout. 3 Venice. 4 Persia. 5 Buddy Holly.
6 A horse. 7 Merlin.

Jackpot Eight.

Quiz 12 answers

....

Round 1

1 Robin Hood. 2 True. 3 St David. 4 The Indian Ocean.
5 Who Dares Wins. 6 Scapa Flow. 7 Eeyore.

....

Round 2

1 The thistle. 2 Glasgow. 3 Ayr. 4 The Grampians.
5 *Ring of Bright Water*. 6 The Picts. 7 The west coast.

....

Round 3

1 An egg. 2 Maraschino. 3 Deer. 4 The pineapple. 5 Manna.
6 A serpent or snake. 7 1853.

....

Round 4

1 Hay. 2 Big Friendly Giant. 3 The USA. 4 Venus. 5 Charles II.
6 Tony Blair. 7 A singer.

....

Jackpot 2000 years.

....

Quiz 13 answers

Round 1

1 A mouse. **2** A dagger. **3** Queen Victoria. **4** Buckinghamshire.
5 None. **6** Romania. **7** The shopping trolley.

Round 2

1 Venice. **2** California. **3** Istanbul. **4** Washington, DC.
5 St Albans. **6** Rio de Janeiro. **7** Birmingham.

Round 3

1 Gryffindor. **2** Dotheboys Hall. **3** Richard Brinsley Sheridan.
4 The Bash Street Kids. **5** *School of Rock*. **6** Billy Bunter. **7** Matilda.

Round 4

1 Mount Kilimanjaro. **2** Stars. **3** 1994. **4** Drivers.
5 Handel. **6** Shelley. **7** Table tennis.

Jackpot The sixteenth century.

Quiz 14 answers

Round 1

1 Sukey. 2 York. 3 Rome. 4 Florida.

5 Wood. 6 Impressive. 7 The Mersey.

Round 2

1 America. 2 Hawaii. 3 Australia. 4 Dr David Livingstone.

5 Apollo 11. 6 Alice. 7 Ferdinand Magellan.

Round 3

1 Mistletoe. 2 *Aladdin*. 3 St Nicholas. 4 1847.

5 Lancer. 6 26 December. 7 An invisibility cloak.

Round 4

1 Australia. 2 True. 3 Surrey. 4 Pumice. 5 Three. 6 The Colosseum.

7 Three (England, Wales and Scotland – as opposed to the United

Kingdom, which includes Northern Ireland).

Jackpot Eighty-eight.

Quiz 15 answers

Round 1

1 Friday. 2 Temperature (accept heat). 3 A bird. 4 *The Simpsons*.
5 Cumbria. 6 The western side. 7 Speak it.

Round 2

1 Shells. 2 Unlucky. 3 Oxen. 4 Irregular. 5 Handwriting.
6 A catapult. 7 Two.

Round 3

1 Two. 2 France. 3 True. 4 A bus or coach.
5 A penny-farthing. 6 Istanbul. 7 London.

Round 4

1 A fawn. 2 January (25). 3 Sri Lanka. 4 Its ears and tail.
5 Norway. 6 Atlantis. 7 False (bees are kept in an apiary).

Jackpot Seven.

Quiz 16 answers

Round 1

1 Ice. 2 Chile. 3 Superman. 4 Light blue and white.
5 Glasgow. 6 An eagle. 7 Huge.

Round 2

1 A dog. 2 The Atlantic. 3 The structure of DNA.
4 Muhammad. 5 Oxford. 6 George VI. 7 George Washington.

Round 3

1 False. 2 South Africa. 3 The Red Sea. 4 Fifty-three.
5 Tigers. 6 (Democratic Republic of the) Congo. 7 The Boer War.

Round 4

1 Dracula. 2 270. 3 Los Angeles. 4 Japan.
5 Oranges. 6 Spanish. 7 Cossacks.

Jackpot 2200.

Quiz 17 answers

....

Round 1

1 Hannibal. 2 Orange. 3 70 per cent. 4 The National Gallery.
5 True. 6 Horses. 7 Japan.

....

Round 2

1 Terriers. 2 *Peter Pan*. 3 Huskies. 4 They do not bark.
5 Snowy. 6 Max. 7 Snoopy.

....

Round 3

1 St Patrick. 2 The (reticulated) python. 3 A forked tongue.
4 True. 5 Medusa. 6 Antarctica. 7 True.

....

Round 4

1 Fairy Liquid. 2 Brer Rabbit. 3 Italy. 4 Oak trees. 5 Everton.
6 True. 7 Violins and other stringed instruments.

....

Jackpot 1958.

....

Quiz 18 answers

Round 1

1 Badminton. 2 Hagrid. 3 The Bay of Biscay. 4 Marco Polo.
5 Darts. 6 Alaska and Hawaii. 7 Snakes.

Round 2

1 Norfolk. 2 *Hollyoaks*. 3 Wiltshire. 4 Scotland.
5 Offa's Dyke. 6 The Severn. 7 In Edinburgh.

Half-time teaser

Some examples are: *Cinderella, Jack and the Beanstalk, Aladdin, Babes in the Wood, Ali Baba, Humpty Dumpty.*

Round 3

1 Thirteen seconds. 2 Israel. 3 George. 4 Air Force One.
5 Japan. 6 Boeing. 7 Concorde.

Round 4

1 False (it is Spanish). 2 The Desert Fox. 3 Russians.
4 A 5p piece. 5 Meat. 6 Cycling. 7 Four.

Jackpot Nine times.

Quiz 19 answers

Round 1

1 Seven. 2 Argentina. 3 A goat and a sheep. 4 A puck.

5 Gerald Durrell. 6 Burned at the stake. 7 Daniel Radcliffe.

Round 2

1 Cinderella. 2 *Shrek.* 3 In a mine. 4 Hansel and Gretel.

5 The Little Mermaid. 6 He climbed up her hair. 7 *Beauty and the Beast.*

Round 3

1 None (they are pawns not prawns). 2 An axe. 3 Yellow.

4 Twenty-two. 5 The king of hearts. 6 Twelve. 7 Four.

Round 4

1 Tagliatelle. 2 Horses. 3 Scooby-Doo. 4 Robinson Crusoe. 5 Sheffield United. 6 Boudicca (or Boadicea). 7 A form of unarmed self-defence.

Jackpot Every fifteen minutes.

Quiz 20 answers

Round 1

1 Rome. 2 Five. 3 Hummingbirds. 4 Football (it was Pelé's nickname).
5 Mother's Day. 6 True. 7 Zurg.

Round 2

1 Ginger Spice. 2 James Blunt (who released 'You're beautiful').
3 Green Day. 4 Mariah Carey. 5 'Waterloo'. 6 All Saints. 7 Beyoncé.

Round 3

1 Noah. 2 The Black Death. 3 Mount St Helens. 4 He was killed and put
in a pie by Mrs MacGregor. 5 Chernobyl. 6 The San Andreas fault.
7 Vesuvius.

Round 4

1 A holt. 2 Queen Victoria. 3 Cycle racing. 4 Nero.
5 Von Trapp. 6 Luxurious. 7 Libya.

Jackpot 30 centimetres.

Quiz 21 answers

Round 1

1 The US president. 2 Omega. 3 Red, white and green.
4 A melon. 5 The Vikings. 6 Karate. 7 France.

Round 2

1 Mars. 2 *Sputnik I.* 3 She became the first Briton in space.
4 Cloud. 5 New Zealand. 6 Jupiter. 7 Eight minutes.

Round 3

1 *The Lion King.* 2 *Futurama.* 3 Dopey. 4 Roger Rabbit (in *Who Framed Roger Rabbit?*). 5 *The Aristocats.* 6 Elmer J. Fudd. 7 Thumper.

Round 4

1 Hercules. 2 Eight. 3 A bull. 4 Four. 5 A musical instrument.
6 Shirley Bassey. 7 Horse racing.

Jackpot 1997.

Quiz 22 answers

Round 1

1 Havana. 2 A heart. 3 Edward VIII. 4 Thirteen.
5 Robbie Williams. 6 The pupil. 7 George III.

Round 2

1 Texas. 2 Truman. 3 A tap. 4 False (they froze in 1932).
5 San Francisco. 6 Louisiana. 7 For answering the telephone.

Half-time teaser

Some possible answers are: batch, hatch, latch, match, patch, snatch, thatch.

Round 3

1 A king or queen. 2 Anti-social behaviour order. 3 Ned Kelly.
4 Martin Luther King. 5 The Gunpowder Plot.
6 Taking (a car) without the owner's consent. 7 True.

Round 4

1 *Charlie and the Chocolate Factory* (and the sequel *Charlie and the Great Glass Elevator*). 2 A rat-like marsupial. 3 Scotland. 4 The Salvation Army.
5 'Open sesame.' 6 World War I. 7 A plant.

Jackpot 90 per cent.

Quiz 23 answers

Round 1

1 The mouse. 2 A statue. 3 Not enough time. 4 Good.

5 Capricorn. 6 E. 7 The Berlin Wall.

Round 2

1 John Constable. 2 Horses. 3 The *Mona Lisa*. 4 Andy Warhol.

5 False (he sold one, entitled *Red Vineyard*). 6 Rembrandt. 7 Madrid.

Round 3

1 Spaniels. 2 A tigon. 3 A butterfly. 4 Eucalyptus leaves.

5 A hare. 6 A spider. 7 True.

Round 4

1 Latin. 2 Porsche. 3 Portsmouth. 4 Thirty. 5 The Gulf Stream.

6 Warwickshire. 7 Hurling.

Jackpot 227.

Quiz 24 answers

Round 1

1 Spain. 2 Jason (and the Argonauts). 3 Northampton. 4 Muhammad Ali.
5 Dublin. 6 A stew. 7 Azkaban.

Round 2

1 A silver lining. 2 A basketball. 3 Florida. 4 Men are six times more likely
to be struck by lightning. 5 Red. 6 Dogs. 7 Katrina.

Half-time teaser

Some examples are: Jonathan (8), Elizabeth (9), Maximilian (10),
Christopher (11).

Round 3

1 Ferrari. 2 Ford. 3 Bluebird. 4 A Volkswagen Beetle.
5 The Highway Code. 6 The bonnet. 7 Liquefied petroleum gas.

Round 4

1 Alfred the Great. 2 Aberdeen. 3 Spiral (or circular).
4 Edgbaston. 5 Cast iron. 6 Naseem Hamed. 7 China.

Jackpot English.

Quiz 25 answers

Round 1

1 Pudding Lane. 2 White. 3 Egypt. 4 A vixen.
5 Alfred Nobel. 6 Furniture. 7 Thirty-five.

Round 2

1 1 January. 2 Hogmanay. 3 First-footing. 4 Robert Burns.
5 Eel. 6 Times Square. 7 Capricorn.

Round 3

1 Spiderman. 2 Captain America. 3 Bruce Wayne.
4 The Incredible Hulk. 5 The Thing. 6 The Penguin. 7 Bananaman.

Round 4

1 Australia. 2 George IV. 3 Two. 4 Jordan. 5 12. 6 Devon.
7 The high jump.

Jackpot 80 per cent.

Quiz 26 answers

Round 1

1 Neverland. 2 180. 3 1945. 4 Italy. 5 *Gladiator*. 6 1967. 7 Captain Nemo.

Round 2

1 Winnie-the-Pooh. 2 *The Man with the Golden Gun.* 3 Robin Williams.
4 Toad of Toad Hall. 5 *Stingray.* 6 *Wuthering Heights.* 7 Mary Poppins.

Round 3

1 Earthquakes. 2 Ninety. 3 Antarctica. 4 A hippo (lives on average thirty years, twice as long as a rhino). 5 Manpower. 6 True. 7 Radioactivity.

Round 4

1 Jamboree. 2 Yellow. 3 Shrove Tuesday. 4 The penguin. 5 A maiden.
6 *Snow White and the Seven Dwarfs* (1937). 7 A monkey.

Jackpot Sixty-eight years.

Quiz 27 answers

Round 1

1 Clark Kent. 2 George Bush (senior). 3 Discworld. 4 False (it is in Morocco). 5 John. 6 The violin. 7 Sleeping sickness.

Round 2

1 Italy. 2 The Scilly Isles. 3 Mauritius. 4 Amity. 5 Sonic the Hedgehog.
6 *Gulliver's Travels*. 7 International Rescue.

Round 3

1 A gosling. 2 By its teeth. 3 Westminster Abbey. 4 A joey. 5 Elizabeth II.
6 The Young Pretender. 7 A calf.

Round 4

1 True. 2 Bell-ringing. 3 Jesus. 4 Polo. 5 One year. 6 Eight. 7 Ham.

Jackpot Greece.

Quiz 28 answers

Round 1

1 *101 Dalmatians.* **2** Cardiff. **3** False. **4** Robert Browning. **5** Jane Austen.
6 Slavery. **7** A venomous snake.

Round 2

1 40–40. **2** Darts. **3** Steve McLaren. **4** Nine. **5** England.
6 The Dragons. **7** Golf.

Round 3

1 Eight. **2** The Round Table. **3** George V. **4** Holyroodhouse.
5 The president of France. **6** John F. Kennedy.
7 Dieu et mon droit (God and my right).

Round 4

1 Moe's. **2** Mary I. **3** The vacuum cleaner. **4** France.
5 Robben Island. **6** Australia. **7** Abraham Lincoln.

Jackpot 21 inches.

Quiz 29 answers

Round 1

1 A typhoon. **2** Blood. **3** Hope. **4** The bouncing bomb. **5** True.
6 The Crystal Palace. **7** Virginia Wade (in 1977).

Round 2

1 New Scotland Yard. **2** Chief Wiggum. **3** Red. **4** Interpol. **5** Lewis. **6** Sun Hill. **7** Black Maria.

Half-time teaser

Some possible answers are: aha, baa, gala, mama, saga, salad.

Round 3

1 To fetch her dog a bone. **2** Doctor Foster. **3** He ran away.
4 Under a haystack, fast asleep. **5** The Grand Old Duke of York.
6 Lucy Locket. **7** School.

Round 4

1 Ali Baba. **2** Butterflies. **3** Fletcher Christian. **4** True.
5 Tina Turner. **6** Romulus. **7** A flying bomb.

Jackpot 1815.

Quiz 30 answers

Round 1

1 Hats. 2 The Czech Republic. 3 Water. 4 Golf. 5 Balaclava (in 1854, during the Crimean War against Russia). 6 Penguins. 7 His heel.

Round 2

1 True. 2 Wellington (the capital of New Zealand).
3 Gold. 4 The *Endeavour*. 5 Yaks. 6 Six. 7 Canberra.

Half-time teaser

Some examples are: McLaren, Maserati, Mazda, Mercedes, Mitsubishi, Morris, Morgan.

Round 3

1 B. 2 Wyoming. 3 Finland. 4 Yuri Gagarin. 5 Beethoven.
6 Catherine Parr. 7 E.

Round 4

1 Fred Flintstone. 2 True. 3 Birds. 4 Russia.
5 Doctor Who. 6 Jonah. 7 A clownfish.

Jackpot Alexandrina.

Quiz 31 answers

Round 1

1 Lean. **2** Cats. **3** Berlin. **4** Judge Jeffreys. **5** *The Wizard of Oz*.
6 Mike Tyson. **7** Richard Nixon.

Round 2

1 Garlic. **2** Bram Stoker. **3** Casper. **4** Hamlet.
5 A poltergeist. **6** Transylvania. **7** Buffy.

Half-time teaser

The complete list is: red, orange, yellow, green, blue, indigo and violet.

Round 3

1 Skirts. **2** The bikini (after the Bikini atoll where atom-bomb testing took place). **3** On your zip (Yoshida Kogyo Kabushikikaisha is the world's largest zip manufacturer). **4** On his chin. **5** Chaps. **6** Inuit (or Eskimo).
7 A deerstalker.

Round 4

1 A rat. **2** The water closet (an early lavatory). **3** Polish. **4** Elizabeth I.
5 150. **6** Bonsai. **7** 180.

Jackpot 1960.

Quiz 32 answers

Round 1

1 Little Miss Muffet. 2 Teeth. 3 The violin. 4 4–2. 5 Chile.
6 11 November 1918. 7 Salzburg.

Round 2

1 Ireland. 2 Ottawa. 3 New Zealand. 4 Malta.
5 France, Belgium and Germany. 6 Norway. 7 Cambodia.

Round 3

1 The Chuckle Brothers. 2 Ambridge. 3 *Strictly Come Dancing*.
4 *The X-Files*. 5 Mr Spock. 6 *Ivor the Engine*. 7 Shilpa Shetty.

Round 4

1 The Danube. 2 Little Tommy Stout. 3 A crossbow.
4 John Wayne. 5 Fifteen. 6 Jerusalem. 7 Central Park.

Jackpot 1940.

Quiz 33 answers

Round 1

1 A fool. 2 13¾. 3 *Mary Rose*. 4 Electric guitar.
5 Jumbo. 6 Russia. 7 Bucharest.

Round 2

1 Mont Blanc. 2 Sir George Everest was Welsh. 3 Rome.
4 *The Sound of Music*. 5 Table Mountain. 6 Scafell Pike. 7 Wimbledon.

Round 3

1 Dick and Dom. 2 Fred Flintstone's. 3 Tweedledee. 4 Laurel and Hardy.
5 Poncho. 6 Yogi Bear. 7 Fred Astaire.

Round 4

1 Iraq. 2 Vincent Van Gogh. 3 True. 4 Dunfermline.
5 G.I. Joe. 6 New York. 7 Moses.

Jackpot 11 per cent.

Quiz 34 answers

Round 1

1 *Billy Elliot*. 2 Hard black. 3 Alex Rider. 4 Russia.
5 John Lennon. 6 Seaweed. 7 Four.

Round 2

1 Women blink twice as much as men. 2 The ear. 3 Red.
4 The eyes. 5 Four. 6 The thumbnail. 7 Canines.

Round 3

1 New Zealand. 2 Icarus. 3 Scurvy. 4 The hovercraft.
5 Bellbottoms. 6 Sir Francis Drake. 7 Denmark and Norway.

Round 4

1 *Neighbours*. 2 An elephant. 3 Black. 4 Figure skating.
5 A donkey. 6 Knots. 7 *The Muppet Show*.

Jackpot 1938.

Quiz 35 answers

Round 1

1 William Shakespeare. 2 Carthage. 3 Eyebrows. 4 A bird. 5 South-west.
6 Horse racing. 7 Kenya.

Round 2

1 Light. 2 Samuel Pepys. 3 *Harry Potter and the Philosopher's Stone.*
4 1994. 5 True. 6 Autumn. 7 Westlife.

Round 3

1 Napoleon. 2 False (whales do not lay eggs). 3 A dog. 4 Sicily. 5 George
Orwell, in his novel *Nineteen Eighty-Four.* 6 Lizards. 7 Giant squids.

Round 4

1 4 July. 2 True. 3 Books. 4 John. 5 Six. 6 A portcullis.
7 Sri Lanka (1960).

Jackpot Julius Caesar.

Quiz 36 answers

Round 1

1 True. 2 Swimming. 3 Mozart. 4 Algeria. 5 True. 6 A hair. 7 Diabetes.

Round 2

1 Bugs Bunny. 2 Lauren. 3 *Blackadder*. 4 Bart Simpson. 5 Robert De Niro. 6 Buzz Lightyear. 7 *The Terminator*.

Round 3

1 Green. 2 The Daleks. 3 Tony Robinson. 4 1958. 5 The Korean War. 6 *Dad's Army*. 7 Newcastle upon Tyne.

Round 4

1 The weather. 2 Siam. 3 Isambard Kingdom Brunel. 4 Handel. 5 In an orchestra. 6 The Netherlands (or Holland). 7 The Anglo-Saxons.

Jackpot 1965.

Quiz 37 answers

Round 1

1 A badger. **2** Twenty-two. **3** The English Civil War. **4** In a piece of music.
5 Moccasins. **6** 168. **7** Golf.

Round 2

1 The Tiber. **2** Scotland. **3** The Ganges. **4** The cinema. **5** True.
6 The Yellow River. **7** Boney M.

Round 3

1 John. **2** Two. **3** J. M. Barrie (in *Peter Pan*). **4** Saigon. **5** Jacobites.
6 Enid Blyton. **7** The Duke of Wellington.

Round 4

1 Pride. **2** Neil Morrissey. **3** Five. **4** For what it's worth. **5** Portugal.
6 Rouen. **7** A locomotive.

Jackpot 1947.

Quiz 38 answers

Round 1

1 Japan. 2 Yellow. 3 A breed of dog. 4 The hermit crab.
5 Personal Best. 6 Maria. 7 Violet Elizabeth Bott.

Round 2

1 Jesse James. 2 John Wayne. 3 Buffalo Bill. 4 A cemetery.
5 Hoover (the others are makers of revolvers). 6 *West Side Story*. 7 True.

Round 3

1 A grape. 2 True (it affects the heart and nervous system).
3 Apples. 4 Nectar. 5 Marie Antoinette. 6 Petrol. 7 Pretzel.

Round 4

1 Australia. 2 Judaism. 3 Brains. 4 Duke. 5 Led Zeppelin.
6 Lyndon Baines Johnson. 7 Madonna.

Jackpot 9 miles.

Quiz 39 answers

Round 1

1 Absence. 2 Fidel Castro. 3 Mercury. 4 St Christopher.

5 Fossils. 6 Three minutes. 7 Outspoken.

Round 2

1 Pegasus. 2 Orange. 3 *Challenger*. 4 The jet engine.

5 *Hindenburg*. 6 Chicago. 7 The bat.

Half-time teaser

Some possible answers are: explain, able, bin, label, pain, lean, pin, axe.

Round 3

1 The Suez Canal. 2 Canada and Mexico. 3 Centaur. 4 The Osmonds.

5 Algeria. 6 Magpies. 7 Asia and Europe.

Round 4

1 The Unready. 2 Cat. 3 10. 4 1998 (France). 5 *Watership Down*.

6 Figure skating. 7 Will Smith.

Jackpot Formic acid.

Quiz 40 answers

Round 1

1 Pisa. 2 F. 3 Alaska. 4 True. 5 Ramsay Street. 6 A board game.
7 Torvill and Dean.

Round 2

1 True. 2 Indonesia. 3 Tenzing Norgay (accept Sherpa Tenzing). 4 Africa.
5 Tibet. 6 Pakistan. 7 The Mediterranean (the others are the South
Atlantic, the North Pacific, the South Pacific and the Arctic and Antarctic
Oceans).

Half-time teaser

Some possible answers are: 10 + 1, 3 + 8, 9 + 2.

Round 3

1 The Rolling Stones. 2 Elvis Presley. 3 Sheffield.
4 Rodgers and Hammerstein. 5 The piano. 6 Beehive. 7 The Sex Pistols.

Round 4

1 A Very Important Person. 2 A school. 3 Four and twenty (24).
4 Silverstone. 5 Eel. 6 Richard I (the Lionheart). 7 Brown, pink and white.

Jackpot 178.

Quiz 41 answers

Round 1

1 David Cameron. 2 *Peter Pan*. 3 A tree. 4 Brazil. 5 George III.
6 With a blast of their trumpets. 7 A killer whale.

Round 2

1 Spain. 2 Lourdes. 3 El Dorado. 4 Westminster Abbey.
5 Las Vegas. 6 Devon. 7 Blackpool (Pleasure Beach).

Round 3

1 The ostrich. 2 An olive branch (accept twig). 3 A cock (or rooster).
4 The phoenix. 5 Canaries. 6 The Navy (the Women's Royal Naval
Service). 7 Wall.

Round 4

1 The Kiwis. 2 Rice. 3 Ethiopia. 4 Samson. 5 Hajj.
6 The Romans. 7 The Seine.

Jackpot Thirty-three.

Quiz 42 answers

Round 1

1 Japan. 2 On a sailing vessel. 3 False. 4 Rugby Union.

5 Fagin. 6 Tex-Mex. 7 Apes or monkeys.

Round 2

1 Hyde Park. 2 Fine tailoring. 3 Westminster Abbey.

4 Blue. 5 Prince Charles. 6 The Tower of London.

7 The Lord Mayor of the City of London.

Round 3

1 Seven. 2 C. 3 The Flying Fortress.

4 One-eighth. 5 Six. 6 1000. 7 Thirteen.

Round 4

1 The rupee. 2 The bittern. 3 Yellow. 4 Galaxies.

5 New Zealand. 6 The US Civil War. 7 Noo Noo.

Jackpot One month.

Quiz 43 answers

Round 1

1 Margaret Thatcher. 2 Donald Duck. 3 Serbia. 4 Tom Sawyer.
5 Weatherfield. 6 Bath. 7 False (it is square).

Round 2

1 An iceberg. 2 Captain Scott. 3 A chopper. 4 Junk. 5 Helen.
6 The *Mayflower*. 7 Portsmouth.

Half-time teaser

Some examples are: aardvark, alligator, ant, antelope, asp, auk.

Round 3

1 14 February. 2 False (she was married to Louis XVI).
3 Brad Pitt. 4 Cleopatra. 5 Venus. 6 Mary, Queen of Scots.
7 Britney Spears (to Jason Allen Alexander).

Round 4

1 Julius Caesar. 2 Red. 3 Wear it. 4 The garden of Gethsemane.
5 Absent without leave. 6 Arthur. 7 They both suffered from poor
eyesight.

Jackpot Three.

Quiz 44 answers

Round 1

1 Paris. 2 Ants. 3 Richard Nixon. 4 Topiary. 5 New York. 6 World War I.
7 *Moby-Dick*.

Round 2

1 Au. 2 Captain Flint. 3 Jesse Owens. 4 Blackpool.
5 An ingot. 6 King Midas. 7 Henry VIII.

Round 3

1 The Pacific. 2 The Thames. 3 La Manche. 4 The Avon.
5 World War I. 6 Narcissus. 7 The gills.

Round 4

1 *Chicken Run*. 2 White. 3 Chelsea. 4 K2. 5 Papyrus.
6 Bangladesh. 7 *His Dark Materials* (by Philip Pullman).

Jackpot Three seconds.

Quiz 45 answers

Round 1

1 Zeus. 2 A donkey. 3 Britain (or England). 4 Fiat.
5 Lancaster (which was a bomber). 6 Angles. 7 Bonnie Prince Charlie.

Round 2

1 Lady Godiva. 2 Alexander the Great. 3 It is the underside of a horse's
hoof. 4 The Grand National. 5 Shadowfax. 6 A beetle. 7 By foot.

Round 3

1 Professor Moriarty. 2 A getaway car. 3 Cruella De Vil.
4 Jack Ruby. 5 *Goldfinger*. 6 Her broomstick. 7 Doctor Black.

Round 4

1 The Three Musketeers. 2 Bedrock. 3 Manchester United.
4 The Atlantic Ocean. 5 Human skin. 6 A buck. 7 Its height.

Jackpot Around 192.

Quiz 46 answers

Round 1

1 A tandem. 2 Seven years. 3 'Dancing in the street'.

4 Cyprus. 5 Normandy. 6 Basketball. 7 Prince Charles.

Round 2

1 Motor and hotel. 2 Sheep. 3 Marmite. 4 A bishop.

5 On board ships (it was a whip). 6 Cricket. 7 Fearful.

Round 3

1 A drummer. 2 A kind of drum. 3 Birmingham. 4 Igor Stravinsky.

5 Charlotte Church. 6 Backstreet Boys. 7 Nelly Furtado.

Round 4

1 Jellystone. 2 Alfred the Great. 3 Timothy Dalton. 4 Monaco.

5 Beatrix Potter. 6 Rabies. 7 Calcutta.

Jackpot 1994.

Quiz 47 answers

Round 1

1 Spaghetti. 2 Candles. 3 An antelope. 4 The *Beagle*.
5 Spanish. 6 Red. 7 *EastEnders*.

Round 2

1 Four. 2 It can run across water. 3 The chameleon.
4 31. 5 The cobra. 6 True. 7 *Animal Farm*.

Half-time teaser

The titles are: *The Philosopher's Stone, The Chamber of Secrets, The Prisoner of Azkaban, The Goblet of Fire, The Order of the Phoenix, The Half-Blood Prince, The Deathly Hallows.*

Round 3

1 Tobacco. 2 Six billion. 3 Pearl Harbor.
4 World War I. 5 Golf. 6 1916. 7 2001.

Round 4

1 A lance or spear. 2 Four. 3 Light. 4 The Wars of the Roses.
5 Jacqueline Wilson. 6 Erwin Rommel. 7 The letter e.

Jackpot 1912.

Quiz 48 answers

Round 1

1 Spiders. 2 True. 3 Welsh. 4 Toy soldiers and animals.
5 A dance. 6 Sand. 7 The trombone.

Round 2

1 A woolly mammoth. 2 New York. 3 King Kong. 4 Turin.
5 *Star Wars* (*The Revenge of the Sith*). 6 A diamond. 7 Toto.

Half-time teaser

Some examples are: Andorra, Belgium, Estonia, France, Greece,
Macedonia, Monaco, Slovenia, Switzerland.

Round 3

1 Q. 2 1000. 3 Louisiana. 4 G. 5 It's the dot above a letter i.
6 Zambia and Zimbabwe. 7 True.

Round 4

1 The shamrock. 2 Queen Victoria. 3 Global Positioning System.
4 The ears. 5 *Three Men in a Boat*. 6 Destiny's Child. 7 Fort Knox.

Jackpot Twenty-six.

Quiz 49 answers

Round 1

1 Aslan. 2 Television. 3 The Royal Mint. 4 Kali.
5 Boxing. 6 Obi-Wan Kenobi. 7 True.

Round 2

1 The Boy Scouts. 2 The FBI. 3 A coven. 4 LA Galaxy.
5 A murder. 6 The Quakers. 7 The Bolshevik party.

Half-time teaser

Some examples are: Samuel Pepys, Pablo Picasso, Pontius Pilate, Marco
Polo, Alexander Pope, Beatrix Potter, Elvis Presley.

Round 3

1 Troy. 2 The Sun. 3 To heat buildings. 4 Barrels. 5 Getafix (Panoramix in
the original French). 6 William I (the Conqueror). 7 Valhalla.

Round 4

1 Lodge. 2 The theatre. 3 Light blue and white. 4 Golf.
5 Canada. 6 Charles II. 7 *The Lost World*.

Jackpot Four.

Quiz 50 answers

Round 1

1 A lake. 2 False (there is more nitrogen than oxygen).

3 Jones (the others were all British prime ministers).

4 Cyclops. 5 Gary Sobers. 6 A small gun. 7 Elizabeth I.

Round 2

1 Sporty. 2 Sharon. 3 Andy Warhol. 4 Elvis Presley.

5 Jordan. 6 Madonna. 7 Beckham.

Round 3

1 Mr Hyde. 2 Sweeney Todd. 3 The escalator. 4 Dartmoor.

5 Rasputin. 6 The Heffalump. 7 *Jaws*.

Round 4

1 Oysters. 2 Charles Darwin. 3 On a ship. 4 An olive wreath.

5 J. K. Rowling. 6 St George's Day. 7 Vicky Pollard (in the TV series *Little Britain*).

Jackpot 80 per cent.

Quiz 51 answers

Round 1

1 At night. 2 Archimedes. 3 Chicane. 4 Billy the Kid.
5 Gauguin. 6 Japan. 7 Christmas.

Round 2

1 Leapfrog. 2 Manchester (the other two are capital cities).

3 A triangle. 4 Nettle (the rest are herbs). 5 Lisbon (the others are in Spain). 6 John Mills. 7 Cluedo.

Round 3

1 The Iron Duke. 2 The Bronze Age. 3 An alloy.

4 Copper. 5 Alchemy. 6 Tin. 7 Platinum.

Round 4

1 Bilbo Baggins. 2 United. 3 Stuart. 4 The Gobi Desert.

5 James I. 6 Australasia. 7 Fingernails (four times faster).

Jackpot 13.6 seconds.

Quiz 52 answers

Round 1

1 A prune. 2 Quidditch. 3 California. 4 Male.

5 Seaweed. 6 The Atlantic and Pacific oceans. 7 France.

Round 2

1 Judy. 2 Two (Anne Boleyn and Catherine Howard). 3 Lenny Henry.

4 Greece. 5 Tatum O'Neal. 6 Michael Douglas. 7 Marge.

Half-time teaser

Some examples are: handkerchief, handle, hand-me-down, hand-out, handyman, secondhand, underhand.

Round 3

1 *A Series of Unfortunate Events* (by Lemony Snicket). 2 By shooting.

3 She was pushed into the oven and roasted alive. 4 Mushrooms.

5 The New Forest. 6 Cleopatra. 7 They had been killed and eaten by an escaped rhinoceros.

Round 4

1 Daffodils. 2 Three. 3 A reindeer. 4 Norway. 5 1936.

6 *The Merchant of Venice.* 7 Eat it.

Jackpot 18 miles per hour.

Quiz 53 answers

Round 1

1 True. 2 Egypt. 3 *Magic*. 4 The Victoria Cross.
5 Baggy trousers. 6 Tennis. 7 150.

Round 2

1 The Mississippi. 2 The Nile. 3 Rowing. 4 The Volta.
5 Art Garfunkel. 6 Belfast. 7 ERIE.

Half-time teaser

Some examples are: Christopher Sproutpants, Johnny Shirtcabbage.

Round 3

1 Black. 2 She was squashed under Dorothy's house. 3 Mildred Hubble.
4 Mickey Mouse. 5 Midnight. 6 The Lady of the Lake. 7 Broomsticks.

Round 4

1 Yellow. 2 Brigadier. 3 Beatrix Potter. 4 Jack the Ripper.
5 A fruit. 6 The goldcrest. 7 In the home.

Jackpot Six.

Quiz 54 answers

Round 1

1 Yeast. 2 Queen Victoria. 3 Polo. 4 Pakistan. 5 Britain.
6 A musical instrument. 7 The port side.

Round 2

1 Switzerland. 2 A piano. 3 The Milky Way. 4 Pullet.
5 Joan of Arc. 6 O. J. Simpson. 7 The Luftwaffe.

Round 3

1 The Garden of Eden. 2 Yard. 3 Capability. 4 Kent. 5 The butterfly bush.
6 Peter Pan's. 7 *The Secret Garden*.

Round 4

1 The conductor. 2 Twelve. 3 The Parthenon. 4 Canterbury.
5 Salty. 6 Portuguese. 7 Jumbo Jet.

Jackpot 1743.

Quiz 55 answers

Round 1

1 The eyes. 2 Sidewalk. 3 Assam (which is a tea; the others are types of coffee). 4 Edward Elgar. 5 Spain. 6 A spy. 7 Bamboo shoots.

Round 2

1 Save Our Souls. 2 Central processing unit. 3 Scuba. 4 District of Columbia. 5 An amphibious vehicle. 6 Mind your own business. 7 Please Turn Over.

Round 3

1 Bob the Builder. 2 *Only Fools and Horses*. 3 Tony Blair. 4 *Who Wants to be a Millionaire?* 5 Bruce Forsyth. 6 *News of the World*. 7 *Enterprise* (in *Star Trek*).

Round 4

1 Biology. 2 The Indian Ocean. 3 Welsh. 4 Mikhail Gorbachev. 5 Mike Myers. 6 In the air. 7 Scotland.

Jackpot 1888.

Quiz 56 answers

Round 1

1 Meat. **2** The Three Musketeers. **3** Fire it. **4** France. **5** *Carousel.*
6 Sacha Baron Cohen. **7** Basketball.

Round 2

1 Her right hand. **2** The Netherlands (or Holland). **3** Twenty-seven.
4 Horses. **5** Herons. **6** The Achilles tendon. **7** Diego Maradona.

Round 3

1 Superman. **2** The Confederates. **3** Potatoes. **4** Sylvester. **5** Al Capone.
6 The mongoose. **7** King Arthur.

Round 4

1 An apple. **2** Loki. **3** Thomas Becket. **4** The Suez Canal.
5 Sir Walter Scott. **6** Ice hockey. **7** The giraffe.

Jackpot 1953.

Quiz 57 answers

Round 1

1 A mountain. 2 TOMORROW. 3 *Prejudice*. 4 Mammals (it resembles a large guinea pig). 5 The Netherlands. 6 The violin. 7 Six.

Round 2

1 Zee. 2 C, O and S (accept U). 3 Royal Automobile Club. 4 Weapons (Special Weapons and Tactics). 5 Liquid crystal display. 6 C. 7 Gemini.

Half-time teaser

256.

Round 3

1 He played his fiddle (more accurately, his lyre). 2 The Nile. 3 Vulcan. 4 In a desert. 5 Lake Superior. 6 A skyscraper. 7 The Atlantic.

Round 4

1 Mecca. 2 Massachusetts. 3 Germany. 4 A squirrel. 5 Iran. 6 Venus. 7 Bats.

Jackpot 1909 (in Letchworth Garden City).

Quiz 58 answers

Round 1

1 Fifty-two. 2 The British Commonwealth. 3 Tutankhamun.
4 Almonds. 5 Weasel. 6 Ben Johnson. 7 Sheep.

Round 2

1 White. 2 The *Marseillaise*. 3 Red. 4 Blue. 5 The USA.
6 The five continents. 7 Trooping the Colour.

Half-time teaser

Some examples are: at, be, by, do, go, in, is, no, on, up, we.

Round 3

1 Nine. 2 Timmy. 3 The owl. 4 The St Bernard. 5 Cerberus.
6 Salem. 7 Curiosity.

Round 4

1 Australia. 2 Lettuce. 3 The Territorial Army.
4 On a mast (usually of a ship). 5 Curling.
6 The Spanish Civil War. 7 False (baboons do have tails).

Jackpot 1981.

Quiz 59 answers

Round 1

1 A pterosaur. 2 Weightlifting. 3 Kenneth Williams.
4 Switzerland. 5 Kuwait. 6 Major. 7 Russia.

Round 2

1 Hindi. 2 *Déjà vu*. 3 A pool. 4 A temporary shelter.
5 A slow dance. 6 Jaffa. 7 A hat.

Round 3

1 A. 2 Cheese. 3 They are all dances. 4 Tom Cruise.
5 *A Midsummer Night's Dream*. 6 Cole Porter. 7 Neville Longbottom.

Round 4

1 A massive tree, otherwise known as the giant redwood. 2 Colombia.
3 Seventeen. 4 The camel. 5 Steak. 6 The *Revenge*. 7 Kenya.

Jackpot Thirty-nine.

Quiz 60 answers

Round 1

1 True. 2 The Louvre, in Paris. 3 Ted Hughes. 4 A goat.
5 Italy. 6 Baseball. 7 A red rose.

Round 2

1 The Caribbean. 2 The Red Sea. 3 The South China Sea.
4 The Mediterranean and the Red Sea. 5 False. 6 The English Channel.
7 On the Moon.

Round 3

1 Krakatoa. 2 Ian Fleming. 3 Bangladesh. 4 A musket.
5 India/Pakistan. 6 The Gunpowder Plot. 7 Basil Brush.

Round 4

1 A fruit bat. 2 The triple jump. 3 Beheaded. 4 Emperor Hirohito.
5 A dance. 6 Augustus. 7 Sausage.

Jackpot 1988.

Quiz 61 answers

Round 1

1 Flowers. **2** Nepal. **3** Beavers. **4** Portugal. **5** *The Nutcracker*.
6 The Farmer's Wife. **7** Three.

Round 2

1 The Clyde. **2** Enid Blyton. **3** The Jordan.
4 Ireland. **5** Tunisia. **6** Greenland. **7** Broadway.

Round 3

1 A private detective. **2** Cat's-eyes. **3** Seals. **4** False.
5 Five. **6** A camel. **7** Circular.

Round 4

1 Snowdon. **2** Red setter. **3** Brown. **4** They were cousins.
5 Sir Alan Sugar. **6** The dock plant. **7** Cricket.

Jackpot 1929.

Quiz 62 answers

Round 1

1 A doe. 2 The piranha. 3 Queen Anne. 4 Zimbabwe.
5 Hiroshima. 6 Tibet. 7 Twenty-eight.

Round 2

1 Halley's Comet. 2 None. 3 Uranus. 4 True.
5 Pluto. 6 Venus. 7 Superman.

Round 3

1 US president Theodore Roosevelt (apparently after he spared a young
bear tied up for him to shoot). 2 True (they are closer to raccoons).
3 In the heavens (they are constellations). 4 Pudsey Bear.
5 The Great Bear. 6 Jack Nicklaus. 7 True.

Round 4

1 Blood. 2 Sir Galahad. 3 Sherlock Holmes.
4 Draws maps. 5 A courgette. 6 Badminton. 7 Tenor.

Jackpot Crete.

Quiz 63 answers

Round 1

1 Two. 2 Arizona. 3 Rugs. 4 A detective. 5 Fire. 6 The hula hoop. 7 False.

Round 2

1 Robinson Crusoe. 2 Madagascar. 3 Cuba. 4 St Helena.
5 Ben Gunn. 6 Hispaniola. 7 Tahiti.

Half-time teaser

Some examples are: Bangor, Barnsley, Birmingham, Bolton, Brighton, Bristol, Burnley.

Round 3

1 Thirteen. 2 Loving and giving. 3 Seven. 4 Good luck.
5 Green. 6 Ireland. 7 The bigger end (or suffer disappointment).

Round 4

1 A boat. 2 The Hudson. 3 Alan Shearer (with 260). 4 Mercury.
5 Oslo. 6 Nepal. 7 A bird.

Jackpot 3 per cent.

Quiz 64 answers

Round 1

1 Pride. 2 A bricklayer. 3 The haka. 4 James I.
5 Anubis. 6 Cricket. 7 The Pentagon.

Round 2

1 The east. 2 Sweden. 3 Tunisia. 4 The Equator.
5 Sudan. 6 The southern. 7 Penzance.

Round 3

1 Darth Vader. 2 Bombay. 3 Chrysalis. 4 Taiwan.
5 Sellafield. 6 John Major. 7 Paul McCartney.

Round 4

1 The UK. 2 New York. 3 Neil Kinnock. 4 A church.
5 The fall. 6 Albania. 7 False.

Jackpot Four.

Quiz 65 answers

Round 1

1 Golf. 2 Terns. 3 Garibaldi. 4 Australia. 5 Spartacus. 6 Stairs. 7 Salt.

Round 2

1 Oscars. 2 *Mary Poppins*. 3 *Jurassic Park*. 4 Private.

5 *Ratatouille*. 6 Sylvester Stallone. 7 Charles Dickens.

Half-time teaser

ARBADACARBA.

Round 3

1 Yew. 2 Palm trees. 3 Milk Wood. 4 The sloth.

5 The horse chestnut tree. 6 An oak tree. 7 The Grand National.

Round 4

1 Robert the Bruce. 2 Paraguay. 3 False (it is a large marine mammal).

4 Sicily. 5 Israel. 6 Humpty-Dumpty. 7 A tuna.

Jackpot 3600.

Quiz 66 answers

Round 1

1 Africa. 2 A technical knockout. 3 Potato. 4 An artist. 5 A flat.

6 The American War of Independence (or American Revolutionary War).

7 Bracket.

Round 2

1 False (they are born all white). 2 He is disqualified. 3 The skunk.

4 The Beatles. 5 Ozzy Osbourne. 6 Greg Norman. 7 Mont Blanc.

Half-time teaser

133.

Round 3

1 Amy Winehouse. 2 Happy. 3 Queen. 4 Robbie Williams.

5 All day long. 6 The Baha Men. 7 The Old Bull and Bush.

Round 4

1 An earl. 2 Calais. 3 On a fingertip. 4 Lord Kitchener.

5 Lord Byron. 6 The Red Cross. 7 France.

Jackpot India.

Quiz 67 answers

Round 1

1 A dance. 2 The French horn. 3 Poland. 4 A bird. 5 Leeds.
6 Lord's. 7 Antarctica.

Round 2

1 The Black Sea. 2 Two. 3 Venezuela. 4 A red admiral (which is a butterfly). 5 Barnacles. 6 Sir Francis Chichester. 7 True.

Round 3

1 Straw. 2 Mortarboard. 3 Father Christmas. 4 A helmet.
5 A bell shape. 6 A sombrero. 7 In a drum kit.

Round 4

1 Rwanda. 2 Minced beef. 3 The Spanish Civil War.
4 A snake. 5 Everton. 6 The tomato. 7 A man.

Jackpot Nine.

Quiz 68 answers

Round 1

1 Mr Funny. 2 *The Canterbury Tales*. 3 Nightwatchman.
4 Philadelphia. 5 George V. 6 10,000. 7 False (it is Arabic).

Round 2

1 Six. 2 Four. 3 A gigabyte. 4 The Great Train Robbery. 5 They are headlands in (North) Wales. 6 Seven. 7 Pinking shears.

Half-time teaser

Some possible answers are: ban, bran, can, fan, flan, pan, span, tan.

Round 3

1 Captain Hook. 2 James Bond. 3 Charles Dickens.
4 Aladdin. 5 Spiderman. 6 Shere Khan. 7 Robin Hood.

Round 4

1 The Red Arrows. 2 Oscar Wilde. 3 The Roman Catholic church.
4 Vincent Van Gogh. 5 The laughing jackass. 6 Paris. 7 Habbakuk.

Jackpot Four.

Quiz 69 answers

Round 1

1 Harold II. 2 Calcutta. 3 58. 4 Vera Lynn. 5 China.
6 Suspected Communists. 7 Animals.

Round 2

1 Haggis. 2 Popeye. 3 Sushi. 4 Breakfast and lunch.
5 A peach. 6 (Rye) bread. 7 Cheese (wrapped in nettles).

Half-time teaser

Some possible answers are: daffodil, dahlia, daisy, dandelion, deadly
nightshade, delphinium.

Round 3

1 The king. 2 False. 3 Nine. 4 Forty-two. 5 Six. 6 Black. 7 Playing cards.

Round 4

1 New York. 2 Corporal Jones. 3 The Congestion Charge. 4 Wilhelm
Richard Wagner. 5 The 800 metres hurdles. 6 Charles Dickens. 7 A vest.

Jackpot Four.

Quiz 70 answers

Round 1

1 *The Wind in the Willows.* **2** Peanuts. **3** Showjumping. **4** Maine.
5 Turkey. **6** Mervyn Peake. **7** A beard.

Round 2

1 Fast (or quick). **2** Morocco. **3** Literate. **4** The stern.
5 Kate Winslet. **6** A lion. **7** Strong.

Half-time teaser

Some possible answers are: dozen, haze, ooze, zebra, zoo.

Round 3

1 Twelve. **2** South Korea. **3** The Yukon. **4** The Forbidden City.
5 Hong Kong. **6** The dragon. **7** The Yellow Sea.

Round 4

1 Little Jack Horner. **2** Belgium. **3** The diamond. **4** Potassium.
5 The Elephant Man. **6** Windsor. **7** Eighteen.

Jackpot 1963.

Quiz 71 answers

Round 1

1 Prima donna. 2 Frans Hals. 3 Two. 4 On a building. 5 *Desire*.
6 On the sea. 7 Mexico.

Round 2

1 A harpsichord. 2 A guitar. 3 The didgeridoo. 4 Bagpipes.
5 Electric guitars. 6 None. 7 A wind instrument.

Half-time teaser

The complete list is: Derbyshire, Devon, Dorset, Durham.

Round 3

1 True. 2 Rabbits. 3 South America. 4 Caligula.
5 Catnip or catmint. 6 Capricorn. 7 Guinea pigs.

Round 4

1 Gas (or gasoline). 2 L. S. Lowry. 3 Aretha Franklin.
4 King John. 5 RHYTHM. 6 Wrestling. 7 Baking bread.

Jackpot 1969.

Quiz 72 answers

....

Round 1

1 Golf. 2 William Blake. 3 Childline. 4 Sandhurst.

5 Germany. 6 Paul McCartney. 7 989.

....

Round 2

1 Tokyo. 2 China. 3 Belgium. 4 Spain. 5 Napoleon.

6 (South) America. 7 Morocco.

....

Half-time teaser

The complete list is: Argentina, Bolivia, Brazil, Chile, Colombia, Ecuador,

French Guiana, Guyana, Paraguay, Peru, Suriname, Uruguay, Venezuela.

....

Round 3

1 Red. 2 Africa. 3 Yellow. 4 Green. 5 Blue. 6 Plants.

7 *Charlie and the Chocolate Factory.*

....

Round 4

1 Fish. 2 Rome. 3 Glasgow Rangers. 4 The Isle of Wight.

5 Nancy Drew. 6 Mary (I). 7 Wine.

....

Jackpot Twenty-seven.

....

Quiz 73 answers

Round 1

1 Squash. 2 A kind of boat. 3 *My Fair Lady*. 4 The Treaty of Versailles.
5 The trumpet. 6 Pakistan. 7 The galley.

Round 2

1 Water. 2 Twenty-five. 3 Volcanoes. 4 Icebergs. 5 Albert Einstein.
6 The atomic bomb. 7 Acid.

Round 3

1 A one-armed bandit. 2 Richard III. 3 The elephant.
4 The Isle of Man. 5 A harp. 6 Eight. 7 Millipedes.

Round 4

1 The gorilla. 2 Rose Tyler. 3 Baseball. 4 Canada.
5 Eagles. 6 A nappy. 7 Apples.

Jackpot 1783.

Quiz 74 answers

Round 1

1 Twenty-four. 2 Heathrow. 3 China or porcelain.

4 Hydrochloric acid. 5 Blenheim. 6 Real Madrid. 7 A plant.

Round 2

1 The secretary bird. 2 The bush. 3 Swans.

4 Alfred Hitchcock. 5 A skate. 6 An albatross. 7 Cygnets.

Round 3

1 Cheese and onion. 2 With the introduction of a hole in the middle.

3 At Easter. 4 Hot dog (accept sausage). 5 A biscuit. 6 Chocolate.

7 Jelly beans.

Round 4

1 *The Mikado*. 2 Charon. 3 Otters. 4 France. 5 Moldova. 6 Tennis. 7 Two.

Jackpot 95 per cent.

Quiz 75 answers

Round 1

1 Barbie. 2 Alfred the Great. 3 Golf. 4 Orchids.
5 Hawaii. 6 Ramadan. 7 366.

Round 2

1 100. 2 Red. 3 The yen. 4 The banknote. 5 Spiders. 6 Poland. 7 Seven.

Round 3

1 Nick. 2 A carnivorous marsupial. 3 Salman Rushdie.
4 St Jude. 5 St James. 6 St Andrew. 7 The Catherine wheel.

Round 4

1 A tree. 2 The knee (it is the kneecap). 3 The Terracotta Army/Warriors.
4 Herring. 5 *Kidnapped* (by Robert Louis Stevenson). 6 Iran.
7 American football.

Jackpot William IV.

Quiz 76 answers

Round 1

1 Plants. 2 A tomato. 3 Brazil. 4 Oscar Wilde.

5 The lungs. 6 Andrew. 7 SEPARATE.

Round 2

1 Three. 2 Four (occasionally, six). 3 Ryan Giggs.

4 Three. 5 Eleven. 6 Italy. 7 Ten.

Half-time teaser

Some possible answers are: underhand, underneath, undo, unexpected, unmask, unplug, unroll.

Round 3

1 Spain. 2 Venice. 3 Scotland. 4 Germany. 5 Czechoslovakia (now divided between the Czech Republic and the Slovak Republic). 6 Venezuela.

7 Greenland won independence from Denmark and left the community.

Round 4

1 *Macbeth*. 2 *The Borrowers* (by Mary Norton).

3 Travis. 4 Crabs. 5 Somerset. 6 111. 7 Kevin.

Jackpot 37°C.

Quiz 77 answers

Round 1

1 Robin Hood. 2 Skiing. 3 Eight (Belgium, Luxembourg, Germany, Switzerland, Italy, Monaco, Andorra and Spain). 4 Flamingos.
5 Two. 6 A barometer. 7 A boat.

Round 2

1 O. 2 The Tower of London. 3 The circulation of blood.
4 Five (eight to nine pints). 5 U2. 6 Arteries. 7 Pluto.

Half-time teaser

Thirty-four.

Round 3

1 On one's head. 2 A ballet dancer. 3 Levi Strauss. 4 Joseph.
5 Liz Hurley. 6 Hans Christian Andersen. 7 A tuxedo.

Round 4

1 Diamonds. 2 Belgium. 3 Nicolas II. 4 Geoff Hurst.
5 Money. 6 The seal. 7 The Emerald City.

Jackpot Chile.

Quiz 78 answers

Round 1

1 Cape Horn. 2 The UK (or England) and France. 3 Cricket.
4 Winds. 5 A type of dress. 6 George Washington. 7 Pocket monster.

Round 2

1 A gander. 2 Sheep. 3 The cow. 4 Cuba. 5 Donkeys. 6 Babe. 7 A kid.

Round 3

1 The Moon. 2 Christopher Columbus. 3 Marco Polo.
4 Journeys into space. 5 Captain Cook. 6 Sir Ernest Shackleton.
7 Neil Armstrong.

Round 4

1 A stamp. 2 Sicily. 3 A singer. 4 Louis XVI. 5 A horse.
6 China. 7 Trainers (or training shoes).

Jackpot India.

Quiz 79 answers

Round 1

1 The Great Barrier Reef. 2 Muttley. 3 The UK. 4 True.
5 Mark Twain. 6 *Jane Eyre*. 7 Topaz.

Round 2

1 Spain. 2 A penguin. 3 Argentina. 4 The Morris dance.
5 A boxer. 6 *Riverdance*. 7 *Strictly Come Dancing*.

Round 3

1 David Hockney. 2 Captain Matthew Webb. 3 Synchronised swimming.
4 The Pacific. 5 Canoeing (or kayaking). 6 150 days. 7 Gargoyle.

Round 4

1 The wedding of Prince Charles and Diana Spencer. 2 Remus. 3 Celtic.
4 Milan. 5 Britain and China. 6 Agatha Christie. 7 Jerusalem.

Jackpot The howler monkey.

Quiz 80 answers

Round 1

1 Africa. 2 Deer. 3 Black. 4 Handwriting. 5 The Impressionists.
6 *Desperate Housewives.* 7 *The Railway Children.*

Round 2

1 Five. 2 'Happy birthday'. 3 Nashville. 4 Five times. 5 Eight.
6 *Top of the Pops.* 7 The Last Post.

Half-time teaser

The complete list is: Bashful, Doc, Dopey, Grumpy, Happy, Sleepy, Sneezy.

Round 3

1 Edward. 2 Agnes. 3 Rasputin. 4 *Dallas.* 5 Florence.
6 The Gandhis. 7 The Royles (in *The Royle Family*).

Round 4

1 Bees. 2 North Atlantic Treaty Organisation. 3 When it is wet.
4 Danish. 5 Sculpture. 6 Linseed. 7 RHUBARB.

Jackpot Saudi Arabia.

Quiz 81 answers

Round 1

1 On a boat. 2 Three. 3 Tchaikovsky. 4 Paris.
5 Sicily. 6 Urals. 7 The hippopotamus.

Round 2

1 Blocks of snow. 2 A church. 3 Lego. 4 A castle.
5 Coventry. 6 London. 7 One.

Round 3

1 A backbone. 2 The funny bone. 3 The leg.
4 The throat (the hyoid bone). 5 Shoulder blade. 6 206. 7 A lobster.

Round 4

1 12. 2 Calamity Jane. 3 A megaphone. 4 Green. 5 The Somme.
6 The British Academy of Film and Television Arts. 7 A mandarin.

Jackpot Peruvian (the others are colours).

Quiz 82 answers

Round 1

1 Oysters. 2 Artists. 3 Oasis. 4 Derbyshire.
5 Aluminum. 6 U-boats. 7 Five.

Round 2

1 Thomas Edison. 2 The ballpoint pen. 3 Rugby. 4 1913.
5 Miners. 6 Wallace (of *Wallace and Gromit*). 7 Trevor Baylis.

Round 3

1 Horse. 2 Goldfinches. 3 ACCOMMODATE. 4 Play it.
5 What you see is what you get. 6 Shoes. 7 Noon.

Round 4

1 Bicycles. 2 Dr Dolittle. 3 Arthur Sullivan. 4 Hungary.
5 The soldier. 6 Panic. 7 Peru.

Jackpot Southend-on-Sea.

Quiz 83 answers

Round 1

1 Thirteen. 2 A sort of metal. 3 HMS *Surprise*. 4 Also Known As.
5 Lewis Hamilton. 6 Horatio Nelson. 7 The jodhpur.

Round 2

1 Peter Shilton (with 125). 2 Gymnastics. 3 Chess.
4 The four-minute mile. 5 South Africa. 6 Jonny Wilkinson. 7 10.

Half-time teaser

The Norman Conquest, the Wars of the Roses, the English Civil War,
World War I, the Cold War.

Round 3

1 Camelot. 2 Graceland. 3 Sherlock Holmes. 4 The Chancellor of the
Exchequer. 5 Manchester United. 6 The Archbishop of Canterbury.
7 Canary Wharf Tower.

Round 4

1 A crater. 2 Edinburgh. 3 Five. 4 Suffolk. 5 Demerara.
6 Timpani. 7 The Koran.

Jackpot George I.

Quiz 84 answers

Round 1

1 A mosque. **2** Four. **3** General Franco. **4** The Rosetta Stone.
5 Russia. **6** *India*. **7** A hard shell.

Round 2

1 New Zealand. **2** Harrison Ford. **3** A small silver bell off Santa's sleigh.
4 *Back to the Future*. **5** Kazakhstan. **6** *Star Trek*. **7** A pig.

Round 3

1 France. **2** The Bastille. **3** Rudolf Hess. **4** Dartmoor.
5 Norman Stanley Fletcher. **6** *Great Expectations*. **7** A search.

Round 4

1 Henry VIII. **2** Naples. **3** Ronald Reagan. **4** The lira.
5 A social blunder. **6** Eat it. **7** The hooker.

Jackpot Prince of Wales.

Quiz 85 answers

Round 1

1 James Bond. **2** False (it is getting bigger due to overgrazing).

3 William Gladstone. **4** World War II. **5** The Wall Street Crash.

6 Women. **7** Play them.

Round 2

1 Daniel. **2** Four. **3** Rugby union. **4** Ursula. **5** Elton John.

6 *The Lion, the Witch and the Wardrobe* by C. S. Lewis. **7** *The Wizard of Oz.*

Half-time teaser

253.

Round 3

1 Nigel Mansell. **2** Sirloin (though it more likely comes from the French *surlonge*, meaning 'above loin'). **3** The dish of the day. **4** Avocado. **5** Cream. **6** Greece. **7** Fish and chips.

Round 4

1 South Africa. **2** (Joseph Mallord William) Turner. **3** South Africa. **4** Agony. **5** A flower. **6** The nightingale. **7** Once.

Jackpot Dancer.

Quiz 86 answers

Round 1

1 50. **2** Alligators. **3** An edible nut. **4** The navy. **5** Israel. **6** Babar. **7** Rice.

Round 2

1 Two. **2** The liver. **3** At the base of one's fingernails.
4 In the neck. **5** Four. **6** Feet. **7** In the head.

Half-time teaser

The complete list is: Edward VII, George V, Edward VIII, George VI and Elizabeth II.

Round 3

1 Michelangelo. **2** Windows. **3** The keep. **4** Mississippi.
5 The hermit crab. **6** Chequers. **7** *Rebecca*.

Round 4

1 Black. **2** Tiger rat. **3** The Trent. **4** She throws herself in front of a train.
5 A plant. **6** Austria. **7** A battle site.

Jackpot California.

Quiz 87 answers

Round 1

1 Banbury Cross. **2** White. **3** Brandy. **4** Davina McCall. **5** Francis Drake.
6 An estate agent. **7** Rhinoceroses.

Round 2

1 The *Victory*. **2** A submarine. **3** *Cutty Sark*. **4** Ballast.
5 Tattoos. **6** A sail. **7** HMS *Belfast*.

Round 3

1 Sunday. **2** Lent. **3** Monday. **4** Saturday (after Saturn).
5 Mercredi. **6** Maundy Thursday. **7** Friday.

Round 4

1 A swarm. **2** A dog. **3** Tennis. **4** The US Civil War.
5 Guinevere. **6** Clouds. **7** Red and white.

Jackpot Sikhs.

Quiz 88 answers

Round 1

1 A turkey. **2** French. **3** Thomas Hardy. **4** An insect.
5 Japan. **6** The Cheshire Cat. **7** £25.

Round 2

1 Elizabeth I. **2** Celtic. **3** Louis Armstrong. **4** Mortimer Mouse.
5 Thomas. **6** President Eisenhower. **7** The Scarlet Pimpernel.

Half-time teaser

Some examples are: baboon, badger, bald eagle, bison, black widow, bream, buffalo, butterfly.

Round 3

1 Reading, writing and arithmetic. **2** Cardinal Richelieu. **3** George III.
4 Third-degree burns. **5** Triceratops. **6** Germany. **7** 633.

Round 4

1 Simple Simon. **2** An African country. **3** Dick Whittington. **4** Ice hockey.
5 Cubic metres. **6** Estonia. **7** A flower.

Jackpot Fourteen.

Quiz 89 answers

Round 1

1 The Browns. 2 Red and green. 3 Benfica. 4 Northern Ireland.
5 Trees. 6 Mahatma Gandhi. 7 Zorro.

Round 2

1 A shooting star. 2 Astronomer Royal. 3 A galaxy. 4 Mercury.
5 False (it is 330,330 times larger). 6 *Futurama*. 7 Polaris.

Half-time teaser

Some examples are: two, three, ten, thirteen, twenty, thirty, two hundred.

Round 3

1 A summer. 2 Mad, or very stupid. 3 Diseases. 4 Buyer beware.
5 To cool your porridge. 6 *Mastermind*. 7 The weather.

Round 4

1 The banana. 2 Finches. 3 Mountains. 4 White. 5 True.
6 Mount Ararat. 7 Eat it.

Jackpot Thirty-six.

Quiz 90 answers

Round 1

1 False. 2 Antlers. 3 *Coronation Street*. 4 True.

5 Princess Margaret. 6 Iran. 7 A snake.

Round 2

1 A dragon. 2 Crete. 3 The unicorn. 4 Beowulf.

5 A mermaid. 6 A bird of prey. 7 The banshee.

Round 3

1 PC Plod. 2 They were hanged. 3 *Bergerac*. 4 Mr Toad.

5 A baton (accept truncheon, its name until the 1990s).

6 The Mounties. 7 Bobby.

Round 4

1 Indiana Jones. 2 Hampshire. 3 Comedians. 4 Amsterdam.

5 In a bed. 6 Seven. 7 March.

Jackpot 13.

Quiz 91 answers

Round 1

1 *Star Wars*. 2 A troop. 3 Afghanistan. 4 Wasps or hornets.
5 Water. 6 Wayne Rooney. 7 Your eyes.

Round 2

1 Cardiff. 2 Cairo. 3 Splatt (which is in Devon in the UK).
4 Manchester. 5 Crystal glass. 6 Istanbul. 7 Los Angeles.

Round 3

1 Atlas. 2 Jeeves. 3 Queen Victoria. 4 John Prescott.
5 The back of a turtle. 6 Passepartout. 7 Batman.

Round 4

1 Origami. 2 The pen. 3 Nothing (both his grandfathers had names
beginning with S and his parents did not want to choose between them).
4 147. 5 Cheese. 6 Napoleon. 7 None.

Jackpot 1800.

Quiz 92 answers

Round 1

1 A jellyfish. 2 The Outlaws. 3 *Absolutely Fabulous*.

4 The USSR (or Soviet Union). 5 Savannah. 6 Unexploded bomb.

7 A fairy tale.

Round 2

1 Red and yellow. 2 Italy. 3 Libra. 4 Thomson and Thompson (Dupond et Dupont in the original French). 5 5000. 6 Greece. 7 Company.

Half-time teaser

12.

Round 3

1 A spider. 2 Beetles. 3 Ants. 4 Termites.

5 The praying mantis. 6 The scorpion. 7 True.

Round 4

1 Yellow. 2 St Valentine's Day. 3 Honda.

4 A sucker. 5 981. 6 Jim Henson. 7 York.

Jackpot Twenty-four days.

Quiz 93 answers

Round 1

1 True. 2 Georgia. 3 Dashes. 4 A scalpel. 5 Blue and white.
6 John Everett Millais. 7 Hydrogen.

Round 2

1 The discovery of penicillin. 2 Smallpox. 3 MEASLES.
4 China. 5 Short-sightedness. 6 Seasickness. 7 The eyes.

Half-time teaser

Some possible answers are: reason, able, son, lean, lob, barn, bale, base,
bean, real.

Round 3

1 Akela. 2 Chairman Mao. 3 Uganda. 4 Genghis Khan.
5 Margaret Thatcher. 6 Joseph Stalin. 7 Brown Owl.

Round 4

1 Faint heart. 2 Rolls-Royce. 3 *Newsround*. 4 Musicians.
5 Pink. 6 Tiananmen Square. 7 A fish.

Jackpot 100.

Quiz 94 answers

Round 1

1 Brown. 2 Canada. 3 Peter Kay. 4 Northampton Town.
5 General Practitioner. 6 Cassius Clay. 7 France.

Round 2

1 Cutlass. 2 A gavel. 3 A bishop. 4 A gardener (it is a wooden basket).
5 The hammer and sickle. 6 Fishermen or anglers. 7 A blacksmith.

Round 3

1 Portugal. 2 Paris. 3 The USA. 4 The Indian Ocean.
5 France. 6 Balmoral. 7 Blackpool.

Round 4

1 Cardiff. 2 Smoke and fog. 3 A sword. 4 Beethoven.
5 George Michael. 6 S. 7 1000.

Jackpot Ewan McGregor.

Quiz 95 answers

Round 1

1 Spain. 2 Eat it. 3 *Star Wars*. 4 P. D. James.
5 Folkestone. 6 Mike Hawthorn. 7 He kissed them.

Round 2

1 The harder they fall. 2 Goliath. 3 Italy. 4 Orpheus.
5 Henry V. 6 Michael Howard. 7 The Red Cross.

Half-time teaser

Some possible answers are: brood, broom, food, good, hoop, kangaroo, roof, room, wood, zoo.

Round 3

1 Big Ben. 2 On a ship. 3 The Seven Dwarfs. 4 Alexander Graham Bell.
5 A handkerchief. 6 Lauren Bacall. 7 Cockneys.

Round 4

1 Anne Robinson. 2 *Lusitania*. 3 The Falkland Islands.
4 Steffi Graf. 5 *Midsomer Murders*. 6 In their neck. 7 Cricket.

Jackpot 265.

Quiz 96 answers

Round 1

1 A sixpence. 2 Norwegian. 3 Investigation. 4 *EastEnders*.
5 Sealed With A Loving Kiss. 6 Web and log. 7 Muggles.

Round 2

1 Hallowe'en. 2 Raymond Briggs. 3 Easter. 4 Mardi Gras.
5 Diwali. 6 364. 7 May Day (1 May).

Half-time teaser

Sean Connery, Roger Moore, Timothy Dalton, Pierce Brosnan, Daniel Craig.

Round 3

1 Carbon dioxide. 2 Starfish (specifically the crown-of-thorns starfish).
3 The Amazon rainforest. 4 The cod. 5 Hybrid car. 6 Forests.
7 London Heathrow.

Round 4

1 RECEIVE. 2 A scream. 3 Champagne. 4 K (at the start of the word).
5 Bats. 6 Hedgehogs. 7 A woman.

Jackpot Tokyo.

Quiz 97 answers

Round 1

1 A shoal. 2 Po. 3 Stalingrad. 4 Grass. 5 Barcelona. 6 None. 7 Please.

Round 2

1 150. 2 Greenwich Mean Time. 3 Stephen Hawking.

4 Bob Dylan. 5 The cuckoo clock. 6 True. 7 The Stone Age.

Half-time teaser

Some possible answers are: Iraq, Mozambique, Qatar.

Round 3

1 The blue whale. 2 Amy Winehouse. 3 Scotland. 4 Picasso.

5 Cats. 6 The Royal Navy. 7 A black hole.

Round 4

1 Green. 2 Judaism. 3 George Washington. 4 Sri Lanka.

5 Habitat. 6 Jean-Claude Van Damme. 7 A herb.

Jackpot   Ten.

Quiz 98 answers

Round 1

1 Three. 2 A bird. 3 Four. 4 Spanish. 5 *Great Expectations*.
6 Edinburgh. 7 Rip Van Winkle.

Round 2

1 The maple leaf. 2 A giant panda. 3 The swastika.
4 Triangular. 5 A cockerel. 6 Copyright. 7 The leek.

Half-time teaser

CHIHUAHUA.

Round 3

1 A dog. 2 The platypus. 3 The flamingo. 4 Birds. 5 Cats.
6 Antelope. 7 The ostrich.

Round 4

1 Butterflies and moths. 2 The North Sea. 3 None. 4 *Bugsy Malone*.
5 Edinburgh (the others are in England). 6 Werewolf.
7 Yellow (accept orange).

Jackpot The *Sun*.

Quiz 99 answers

Round 1

1 Australia. 2 The British Army. 3 Tea. 4 New York. 5 Garlic.
6 A rake. 7 Play it.

Round 2

1 Florence Nightingale. 2 New Orleans. 3 Saddam Hussein.
4 The Springboks. 5 John Wayne. 6 Tommy. 7 Chicago.

Half-time teaser

Some possible answers are: drop, flop, lop, plop, stop, top, swap.

Round 3

1 Cairo. 2 Berlin. 3 The Thames. 4 Rome. 5 Venice. 6 Paris. 7 Disneyland.

Round 4

1 Upwards. 2 Votes for women. 3 A table. 4 The screwdriver (the others
are torture devices). 5 Dundee (in *Crocodile Dundee*). 6 Fungus. 7 Corgis.

Jackpot Loughborough (for a temperance meeting).

Quiz 100 answers

Round 1

1 Nectar. **2** Arnold Schwarzenegger. **3** Nuclear weapons.
4 Crows. **5** Liverpool. **6** Actors. **7** Vet.

Round 2

1 The Fens (the other two are mountain ranges). **2** *Swallows and Amazons* (the other two are books about Alice by Lewis Carroll). **3** Damien Hurst (the other two are poets). **4** Macedonia. **5** Ghana (the others are in South America). **6** An apple. **7** Chorister (the other two are lawyers).

Half-time teaser

Some possible answers are: Algeria, Angola, Chad, Congo, Egypt, Mali, Nigeria, Zambia, Zimbabwe.

Round 3

1 Admiral Horatio Nelson. **2** Julius Caesar. **3** *King Kong*.
4 Henry VIII. **5** *Gone With the Wind*. **6** Beethoven. **7** Charles II.

Round 4

1 Red and white. **2** Jane Austen. **3** On a digital image or computer screen.
4 Goats. **5** Cars. **6** The Circus Maximus. **7** Blue.

Jackpot A shoe.

Quiz 1 for Grannies and Grandpas answers

Round 1

1 The Boer War. 2 Gene Kelly. 3 Hans. 4 *The Man from UNCLE*.
5 A tie. 6 *A Christmas Carol*. 7 1947.

Round 2

1 Princess Royal. 2 Seventeen. 3 Canute. 4 George VI. 5 True.
6 Wallis Simpson. 7 1981.

Round 3

1 D-Day (6 June 1944). 2 Clementine (Clemmie). 3 Overlord.
4 Mussolini. 5 Vichy France. 6 The Mods. 7 1982.

Round 4

1 The Pyramids of Egypt. 2 Spies. 3 Rocky Marciano. 4 Noel Edmonds.
5 A litre bottle. 6 A quarter of an old penny. 7 New tricks.

Jackpot 1983.

Quiz 2 for Grannies and Grandpas answers

Round 1

1 Bob Hope. 2 In the dining room. 3 Meccano. 4 True.
5 'A hard day's night'. 6 A tennis player. 7 The ball burst.

Round 2

1 Elvis Presley. 2 On a person's head (it was a hairstyle). 3 Johnny Cash.
4 Rhythm and blues. 5 Cliff Richard. 6 1931. 7 'All shook up'.

Half-time teaser

The complete list is: Winston Churchill, Anthony Eden, Harold
Macmillan, Alec Douglas-Home, Harold Wilson, Edward Heath, Jim
Callaghan, Margaret Thatcher, John Major, Tony Blair and Gordon
Brown.

Round 3

1 Monopoly (in 1931). 2 A spanner. 3 White.
4 The eighteenth century. 5 Mayfair. 6 Checkers. 7 88.

Round 4

1 Forty. 2 *Countdown*. 3 1971. 4 West Ham.
5 A yard. 6 A sewing machine. 7 Amnesia.

Jackpot 1893.

Quiz 1 for Mums and Aunties answers

....

Round 1

1 The Amazons. **2** *Rebecca*. **3** King John. **4** (TV) chefs.
5 Two (Ruth and Esther). **6** Joey. **7** Sindy.

....

Round 2

1 *Emmerdale*. **2** 1985. **3** Charlene Mitchell (or Charlene Robinson).
4 The Bull. **5** Status Quo. **6** *Brookside*. **7** *Hollyoaks*.

....

Round 3

1 Fourteen. **2** Felix Mendelssohn. **3** Three French hens. **4** Scarlett O'Hara.
5 Auguste Rodin. **6** She sent the first known Valentine card. **7** Sixty.

....

Round 4

1 Chocolate. **2** T. Rex. **3** Omar Sharif. **4** 45 minutes.
5 *The Waltons*. **6** Scotland. **7** Beanie Babies.

....

Jackpot 1904.

....

Quiz 2 for Mums and Aunties answers

Round 1

1 Birmingham. 2 The burka (or chador). 3 Before birth. 4 1984.

5 *Anne of Green Gables* (and its sequels, including *Anne of Avonlea*).

6 T. S. Eliot. 7 Blue.

Round 2

1 Squid. 2 Sweden. 3 A hairdresser. 4 Chickpeas. 5 Tarragon. 6 Sausages.

7 Prawns.

Round 3

1 Juan Fangio (who was a racing driver). 2 Leather bags. 3 Shoes.

4 David and Elizabeth Emanuel. 5 Horse racing. 6 Paul McCartney.

7 A boa.

Round 4

1 The third finger of the left hand. 2 A pacifier. 3 (All one's) eggs.

4 Good Friday. 5 The Body Shop. 6 Wear it. 7 Carbonara.

Jackpot Three months.

Quiz 1 for Dads and Uncles answers

Round 1

1 Scott Tracy. 2 The Doors. 3 Jimmy Greaves. 4 2007. 5 A drill.
6 *Are You Being Served?* 7 A wine bottle (a worm is another name for a corkscrew).

Round 2

1 Sunderland. 2 Gold. 3 Wrestling. 4 Tiger Woods.
5 Thirteen. 6 Four. 7 The gridiron.

Round 3

1 Fiat. 2 A microlight. 3 The Soviet Union. 4 1959. 5 Yellow.
6 The Isle of Man. 7 Aston Martin.

Round 4

1 Nirvana. 2 Bruce Willis. 3 Green. 4 David Bowie.
5 1956. 6 Captain Black. 7 *Playboy*.

Jackpot 1925.

Quiz 2 for Dads and Uncles answers

Round 1

1 Celtic and Rangers. **2** U2. **3** The Angels. **4** George Harrison.
5 Ronseal. **6** Thailand. **7** The Bermuda Triangle.

Round 2

1 *Carry On Sergeant.* **2** *Reservoir Dogs.* **3** Clint Eastwood.
4 Batman (he was the Penguin). **5** A submarine. **6** The US Civil War.
7 Catwoman.

Half-time teaser

Some examples are: **Barnsley, Birmingham City, Blackburn Rovers, Bolton Wanderers, Brentford, Bristol City, Burnley, Bury.**

Round 3

1 The Rovers Return. **2** Carlsberg. **3** Rum. **4** Mary I. **5** Pears.
6 Ginger ale. **7** 1853.

Round 4

1 A great white shark. **2** France. **3** *The Magic Roundabout.* **4** Uruguay.
5 Two. **6** The Parachute Regiment. **7** Lieutenant Commander 'Scotty' Scott.

Jackpot 1871.

Quiz 1 for Teens answers

Round 1

1 Santa's Little Helper. 2 KFC (Kentucky Fried Chicken).

3 General Certificate of Secondary Education. 4 Hawaii.

5 A stingray. 6 France. 7 Alton Towers.

Round 2

1 Kylie. 2 Scotland. 3 Lily Allen. 4 Simon Cowell.

5 Justin Timberlake. 6 Green Day. 7 The Stereophonics.

Round 3

1 *Wardrobe*. 2 *The Lord of the Flies*. 3 Gryffindor.

4 *The Catcher in the Rye*. 5 Terry Pratchett. 6 Mr Jones. 7 *Eragon*.

Round 4

1 Rembrandt. 2 Wipe-out. 3 Christopher Eccleston.

4 Neuf. 5 Black. 6 *Oliver*. 7 On Jupiter.

Jackpot Eleven.

Quiz 2 for Teens answers

Round 1

1 Hinduism. 2 Base jumping. 3 Frodo. 4 A friend.
5 360. 6 23.50. 7 Sixteen.

Round 2

1 Sony. 2 Get a life. 3 A mouse. 4 Computer-generated imagery.
5 2001. 6 Frequently Asked Question(s). 7 *Grand Theft Auto*.

Round 3

1 *Black Pearl*. 2 Hawaii. 3 *High School Musical*.
4 The Crystal Skull (of Akator). 5 *Toy Story*. 6 Lara Croft. 7 Imhotep.

Round 4

1 True. 2 26. 3 Real Madrid. 4 Mort. 5 A brachiosaurus.
6 True. 7 Roald Dahl.

Jackpot 1800 times.

Quiz 1 for Under-10s answers

Round 1

1 Sugar and spice and all things nice. **2** Gordon. **3** 100.
4 5 November. **5** A fly. **6** Trafalgar Square. **7** Three.

Round 2

1 An ostrich. **2** Bees. **3** Tadpole. **4** The cheetah.
5 Bambi (the others are bears). **6** The giraffe. **7** True.

Round 3

1 Princess Fiona. **2** *The Jungle Book.* **3** *Monsters Inc.* **4** Minnie Mouse.
5 *The Little Mermaid.* **6** *Transformers.* **7** *The Incredibles.*

Round 4

1 Outside. **2** A foal. **3** The Sun. **4** A hedgehog. **5** Four. **6** When water is
poured on his head. **7** Prince Philip (or the Duke of Edinburgh).

Jackpot The Tip and Run.

Quiz 2 for Under-10s answers

Round 1

1 Sixty. 2 The porcupine. 3 One (February).

4 Sleet. 5 A doctor. 6 Blood. 7 Horrid Henry.

Round 2

1 Paris. 2 Everest. 3 Jamaica. 4 The Pacific Ocean.

5 New York. 6 Wales. 7 Los Angeles.

Round 3

1 Some tarts. 2 A swan. 3 He blew them in (or down).

4 *Jack and the Beanstalk*. 5 The fox. 6 Goldilocks. 7 His crown.

Round 4

1 Seven. 2 Be prepared. 3 Six. 4 *The Lion King*.

5 A fleece. 6 Yellow. 7 Pharaohs.

Jackpot The pterodactyl.

Answer sheet

Team name

Round 1

1

2

3

4

5

6

7

Round 2

1

2

3

4

5

6

7

Half-time teaser

Round 3

1

2

3

4

5

6

7

Jackpot

Total

Round 4

1

2

3

4

5

6

7